Your Family Matters

Advance Praise for *Your Family Matters*

"Making parental decisions is not easy and now with everything that our children are exposed to and the stress and challenges facing parents today, it is good to have resources like Dr. Kanner's book *Your Family Matters* is a full-range, no-subject-off-limits kind of resource on parental decision making."

— Larry King, Host of *Larry King Live*

"The challenges of parenting have changed dramatically from what I refer to as the "great generation" There are so many more distractions for our children between cyberspace activity and virtual reality that parents today have a bigger challenge in preparing their children to be active participants in society. It is so encouraging to see all of the proven and very current tools Dr. Keith Kanner provides for parents with children of all ages."

— Jenny Craig

"In our effort to support our children grow their self esteem and become engaged members of their communities, we rely on solid, practical and professional advice from highly regarded experts. Dr. Kanner definitely tops that list. Your Family Matters is a comprehensive parenting resource covering a wide range of topics that are both timely and timeless. It's the How To encyclopedia of common parental dilemmas."

— Joani Wafer, Co-Founder and CEO,
Kids Korps USA

"Dr. Kanner has tackled some of the most difficult issues facing parents and children with clear and concise answers The FAQ's section at the end of each chapter helps personalize the information for your child. This book should be part of every parent's library."

— Dr. Stuart Rubenstein

Your Family Matters

Solutions to Common Parental Dilemmas

Dr. Keith Kanner

Your Family Matters ©2011 by Dr. Keith Kanner

Love Your Life Publishing, Inc
7127 Mexico Road Suite 121
Saint Peters, MO 63376
www.LoveYourLifePublishing.com
publisher@LoveYourLifePublishing.com

ISBN: 978-1-934509-32-6

Library of Congress Control Number: 2010935078

Printed in the United States of Amercia

Cover Design by: www.MonkeyCMedia.com

Internal Design: www.Cyanotype.ca

First Printing: 2011

Author Contact: www.Kanner.tv

TABLE OF CONTENTS

DEDICATION

To my parents, Edwin and Penny Kanner: I was blessed to be brought up by two highly educated professionals who were also equally devoted to their families. They were the impetus for making my family so important to me as well as for pursuing my professional passion. They were great role models on how to balance being a professional and a parent very early in my life.

To my children, Kassidy, Christopher, and Zackary, who are the best teachers of how to be a great father. They make me want to be the best father I can be. I wish for each of them to aspire towards picking a profession that they have a passion for and always making their families come first.

ACKNOWLEDGEMENTS

WHERE I AM IN MY CAREER AS WELL AS THE accomplishment of this book could not have happened without the love and support of many people. To all my friends and colleagues for their unconditional encouragement, I wish I could list all of you!

To Richard Doutre Jones from Fox and XETV for being a visionary mentor. Richard's consistent belief and support of me and how I help people was the driving force for getting me where I am today in terms of the media aspect of my profession. Developing and building the brand of Your Family Matters into two shows, which led to awards and a national audience, Richard continues to be a driving force behind my wish to help as many people as I can better understand and raise their children to be happier and healthier.

To Cindy Ford for being my agent and believing in me from the very beginning. Cindy supported and encouraged me to bring my book and my brand to the national media platform. With her guidance Your Family Matters will continue to make its mark on the television, internet, and radio marketplace.

To Monkey C Media for the creative design talents they brought to the book cover and the website, www.kanner.tv

To Paul Menard, my radio guru and executive producer for Your Family Matters with Dr. Keith Kanner radio show sponsored by Sylvan Learning. Paul inspires me to continually bring new ideas to the show.

To Dr. Calvin Colarusso, my colleague, confidant and Yoda. Cal encouraged me to use my skills to convert developmental and psychoanalytic theory into a medium that is easily understood by the general public so they can use it to better their lives and the lives of their families.

To Lee Sorenson and Sylvan Learning for being a great National Sponsor.

To Dr. Alan Sugarman and my colleagues at both the San Diego Psychoanalytic Society & Institute as well as my fellow Professors in the Department of Psychiatry at U.C. San Diego who are essential in continuing to educate young doctors and clinicians in helping children, adolescents, and parents live healthier and happier lives through education and treatment.

To John Assaraf for his friendship, support and encouragement. I am looking forward to collaborating with him on future books including *My Father, The Jewish Mother.*

FOREWORD

BY JOHN ASSARAF

AS A PARENT OF TWO VIBRANT, HEALTHY, AND STRONG-minded boys aged 13 and 14, I pride myself on being a great dad. That of course is my ego wanting to be a great dad. The truth is my intentions and my reality sometimes don't match up. We all have hopes and dreams of being great parents, however many of us are learning how to parent by trial and error.

For many years I thought that because I was a boy once (still am at heart) it would be easy for me to understand what my kids were thinking, experiencing, and going through. Although that may be the case in a few areas, their willingness to allow me into their world wasn't as easy as I had hoped. I thought I understood their emotions, feeling, desires, fears and insecurities. I didn't.

What they are experiencing is and isn't what you or I went through. Mother Nature and genetics have a way of mixing and matching the characteristics, likes, dislikes, features, attitudes and propensities in so many ways, we are really shooting in the dark thinking we know our kids and how to navigate the parenting waters. From the discussions I have with my friends, this situation is not only normal it seems to be the norm in varying degrees for all of us who truly want to be wonderful, loving parents.

Several years ago I was at a total loss as to how to understand what one of my son's was experiencing and expressing. The harder I tried to do what I thought was right, the worse off I made the situation. For a short period of time, my heart was saddened and my attitude weakened thinking I was failing my child.

I tried everything I thought would work, however I just didn't try everything there was to try because I didn't know what I didn't know. I think many of us parents follow our hearts and our own experiences thinking we are doing our best. Sometimes the best we know isn't good enough.

In my book, *The Answer*, I talk about the importance of seeking out help for areas where you don't yet know you need help. How is that possible if you don't know you need it? Simple: you *assume* you don't know and you reach out to professionals who have more experience in those areas and can provide you with resources you might not have access to otherwise. If you want to achieve anything greater in your life than your current circumstances, whether it is being an exceptional parent or extraordinary business leader, you need to acquire more knowledge and improve your ability to ask for help.

When I applied this same concept to my own situation, I knew it was time to seek out the help of someone highly skilled in the psychology of parenting. That's when I met Dr. Keith Kanner. A friend recommended I seek out his council and thank GOD I listened. I set aside my know-it-all-attitude and put on my learn-it-all-attitude and began a quest to learn how to understand my son's thoughts, feelings and attitude. After several private sessions with Dr. Kanner and several with my son together, we both started to understand each other's vantage point and we learned skills to communicate at a level we didn't have before. It was truly wonderful to learn a new set of tools to simplify my father-son relationship.

As I reviewed the content within this book, I quickly realized again that I have so much to learn and I needn't go far for the tools and answers. They are all here now. This book contains within it the passage to freedom, peace, and love with your child. As you know, application of the right information in the right order is a surefire way to succeed in any area of life.

This book has within it pearls of wisdom, tools, tactics, and specific knowledge that will transform your life with your kids forever.

Parenting is like every one of life's wonderful gifts: it provides us the opportunity to grow and learn from those who play at the things we have to work at. This book will help you play at parenting and show you the path to being a great role model to your kids. The rewards, as you can imagine, are priceless.

I wish you all the joys that only being a parent can offer.

JOHN ASSARAF,

- New York Times Bestselling Author, *The Answer* and *Having It All.*
- Featured in the blockbuster movie and book *The Secret.*
- CEO, OneCoach.

INTRODUCTION

ME FIRST? KIDS FIRST?

AT THE TIME OF THIS WRITING, WE ARE EXPERIENCING a significant paradox. While we are living in the "Me" generation, implicit in "taking care of oneself first", many of our children are suffering. We have all heard the common adage, "You can't take care of others if you don't take care of yourself first." True, but this concept has been taken out of context and it has led to declines in both children's mental health and increases in selfish thinking.

Many viewers of my television show have contacted me with grave concerns about how good parenting has fallen due to increases in both personal and materialistic thinking over the past ten years. Sociologists and social psychologists have taught us that changing societal standards trickle down to generational shifts in terms of how certain rules and laws perpetuate standards. Common routines and social influences follow in step, including family values. Exercise programs, crash dieting, makeovers, and other "me-related" advents have replaced the emphasis on families and the children and parents' need to make the investment into their children *before* anything else.

What happened to the age-old concept that children SHOULD come first? Decades of research have documented the importance of a parent's investment in their children's lives with proven data showing that the parents who are the most invested in their children, especially during infancy through the grade school years, tend to produce the healthiest offspring. I have always found it amazing that even on airplanes we are told "If there is a loss of cabin pressure, put your oxygen mask on before your child's." Almost every invested parent I know would focus on calming their child down and attending to them first before worrying about themselves. One mother told me it would be the same if her child was drowning in a pool — you hold your breath, jump in, and save your child — it's a no-brainer. But is it? For some parents perhaps it is, but not for all.

As with any society, there are a multitude of influences and new trends challenging common sense and even good parenting. I agree with the concept that people need to take good care of themselves, but if you don't put your children before anything else in your life, you fail them and you fail yourself. Unlike other animals, the human infant is completely dependent upon their caregivers for survival; the essence of parenting and protection should not stop until the child has been able to take over those parental functions independently. Typically this does not happen until the child leaves home for college or work, and even then parents are still needed.

So, how does one integrate societal shifts and maintain optimal parenting to assure that the welfare of their child is not compromised?

1. Kids must come first. There seem to be two types of people: those who place themselves first, and those who place their children first. I have serious concerns for any parent who would place their needs before a child's. In fact, I believe we need to educate children, adolescents, and young adults earlier about the necessity of parental commitment before they consider beginning a family. This training would include the concepts of selflessness, child development, and the amazing joys of parenting done the right way. Over the past 15 years there have been more parenting classes offered, not for NEW parents, but for parents who struggle with their kids. If parental education started earlier we would all be better off. Perhaps taking a look into the future would provide a more informed choice about becoming a parent; those thinking it's not for them might wisely choose not to go down that path in life.

2. Use your parental intuition. Most parents have the right intentions, but sometimes don't trust themselves based on what other people say or do. For example, I have had numerous parents tell me they sometimes feel like "the bad guy" for placing limitations on their children as compared to other parents. This puts them in a conflict and they often give in, which leads to common problems.

3. Educate yourself about child development. Having a roadmap is always the way to go or you are going to get lost. Children and adolescents are complicated and change from stage to stage. If you learn why and what to do, life is easier for everyone.

4. Listen to your kids. As parents, we tend to talk more than we listen. When we listen to our children, we learn where they are at, what they feel, and most importantly, what they need from us. But, we must listen without being judgmental or they won't talk to us. You will have your time to guide — just let them finish first.

5. Play with your kids. We are all busy, especially now living in a recessed economy. We are all working harder than ever, but we still need to remain present and available to our children. I am currently volunteering every day at lunch at my son's school to coach and play football with him and his friends. It is the most rewarding part of my day. Not only do I ensure they have fun, get exercise, share, take turns, and learn some football skills, but they all teach me about what their worlds are like — it helps me help them.

6. Family time. Whether your family is intact or not, family is still family. Even in dual households, family traditions are essential and will last a lifetime. Family dinners every night, a reading hour, a game night, joint exploration — it doesn't matter what you do, just do it, and do it on a regular basis.

7. Balance is key. Extremes cause problems. Angry and selfish parents produce angry and selfish children. Parents who understand the true essence of parenting see this as their most important investment in the world and they plan accordingly. Working out is necessary, but *after* the kid's needs are taken care of.

It is easy to get lost in the exhausting, yet wonderful world of parenting. Those of us who place our kids first will affirm that being a mom or dad is the greatest of G—s gifts to us. But this time goes by really fast. The healthier our children, the faster they separate from us and leave us for their friends. Enjoy it before it's too late. There will be plenty of time for "Me" once they leave home. In fact, for all you great parents out there, developing activities to help us mourn the loss of parenting will be welcomed and needed.

CHAPTER 1

SIGNS OF KID BURNOUT

Ten year old Brian has always been considered a high achiever. Historically an excellent student and athlete, both he and his parents have consistently expected pristine performance and compliance toward any activity to which Brian dedicated himself. In a typical year, aside from a challenging academic day, Brian has also been involved in multiple activities both after school and on the weekends. Last year he played after-school soccer, attended piano and guitar lessons every week, took Spanish lessons, and was involved in his church group. Brian and his parents had been equally invested in his "busy" schedule. The only complaints Brian ever made were that he had very little time to spend with friends and that he never really had any time to "just relax." Like most children eager to please their parents, Brian's occasional complaints were only subtly voiced and went unnoticed by his parents.

This type of scheduling had been habitual behavior for Brian since he was four years old. His parents had always taken pride in Brian's accomplishments and Brian initially felt a sense of pride in his busy schedule. This year, however, some changes in his behavior were observed and concerns were raised by two of Brian's teachers. Brian's mood and attitude seemed to significantly shift about a month into the school year. His typical high spirits and level of participation had been replaced with a sense of flatness and fatigue. His head was often seen slumped, and his body language was described as "droopy." The quality of his work was slipping from superior to average, and he had seemed to lose his usual love of school. At home Brian became resistant to piano and guitar practice, and his soccer coach told his parents he seemed to be "in outer space" when on the field. Such radical changes were discussed between Brian and his parents and the only thing Brian could acknowledge was that he felt really "tired" and did not feel well.

This example highlights a common condition referred to as "Kid Burnout." Familiar in the literature are studies about adult conditions of occupational burnout, but very little has been researched or written about this condition in children and adolescents. Despite the legitimacy of child burnout, parents and educators tend to overestimate how much kids can or should have on their plates, often supplementing quality with quantity.

The general cause of burnout is due to an over-extension in one's capacity to function normally. When this level has been reached (which is highly subjective depending upon who you speak to) psychological and physical symptoms develop. These symptoms can be as subtle as mood changes leading to more significant conditions such as physical illness. Ironically, allowing children to carry heavy schedules is a well-intentioned effort to expose them to a wide range of activities to enrich their lives. In fact many times high energy children ask for more and more and their parents sign them up for additional activities to make them happy. Yet when their children become disgruntled about disliking the activity they wanted so badly, the parents feel guilty.

As discussed in adult literature, burnout is avoided through achieving balance in one's life.The difference with adults and children, however, is that children usually do not have the capacity to balance themselves. They need their parents to use intuition and experience to decide what constitutes good balance, even at the potential displeasure of their child. It is better to have a child experiencing short-term disappointment than suffering long-term burnout. Parents need to demonstrate balance in their own lives for children to observe and demonstrate.

Key Points:

1. **Parents need to consider quality over quantity when scheduling activities for their children.**
2. **Children need time to just relax.**
3. **Parents need to set an example of a balanced schedule.**
4. **"Kid Burnout" is often a result of well-intentioned parents aiming to expose their children to a variety of activities.**
5. **It is the responsibility of the parent to set and manage their child's schedule and make necessary adjustments.**
6. **Major signs of "Kid Burnout" include:**
   - **Personality changes;**
   - **An unusual lack of interest;**
   - **Sadness or apathy;**
   - **Consistent fatigue;**
   - **Attention problems;**

- **Changes in quality of performance;**
- **Complaining.**

FAQ's

1. *What role should children play in creating their schedule?*

Children should be actively involved with creating their schedule, which will decrease animosity, if any, towards their parents. Although parents might have particular activities they want their child to participate in like playing sports or a musical instrument, or another extracurricular activity, the child needs to be able to choose the specific activity within that category. For instance, a parent might tell their child they think they should play a sport because it is healthy for them, but giving the child the option of which sport to play is a nice compromise. If the subject is approached this way you will get far less resistance from your child than if you simply say, "I was a football player, so you should be one also." Therefore it is more important to ask which activity your child wishes to participate in rather than *if* they want to participate.

2. *What steps should a parent take to address a child who is experiencing burnout?*

- The parent should self identify whether they think their child is burning out;
- The parent should determine what they themselves think burnout out is and how burnout would make them feel;
- The parent should go to their child and without asking the child, make a statement based on what they are hearing or seeing. For

instance, "You appear less interested in going to your ballgames or playing your guitar, and it looks like you are struggling with finding time to spend with your friends."

- The parent should ask the child what they can do to help them get through it;
- If/when the child or adolescent acknowledges burnout is happening, parent and child should collectively come up with an agreed upon plan, addressing the burnout while at the same time being very connected to the inner feelings of the child (i.e., the child is tired, frustrated, bored; they are having a hard time delaying gratification of summer or a holiday coming up etc.). The more the child can understand that the parent knows what burnout is like and has had their own experiences, the less alone the child will feel and the more connected to their parent.

3. ***Given the competitive nature of our environment, how should parents rationalize having their children do less?***

The parent must take the developmental age of child into consideration. Introducing competitive sports to children who are under the age of eight is not a good idea developmentally because they are already dealing with internal issues of winning, losing, and fairness. If wrapped into another event such as a competitive sport, this may be too much for them and may actually deter the child in the long run from playing competitive sports. Parents need to be able to resist the urge to have their child participate in what everyone else's child is doing, and instead take responsibility for what they believe is best for their child and work within those guidelines.

If your child is in a competitive atmosphere or one that may be too competitive, you need to actively try to help the child not take the activity too seriously or to the point where it may inadvertently hurt both their ego and their performance capabilities. Until late childhood, namely 11 years old to pre-adolescence, fine and gross motor skills are still developing. Therefore there are only certain capabilities many children will be able to accomplish. This does not mean there are not children who are gifted athletes or a natural phenomenon, such as Tiger Woods for example.

I would encourage parents to talk to other parents and coaches about the normalization of not being overly competitive too early. The more people speak up about what is healthy and normal, the more others will follow. By standing up for the developmental health of the child, and not succumbing to the belief that without these competitive sports/activities the child might be teased in school, the parent has the ability and the opportunity to really educate people on this subject.

CHAPTER 2

SOCIALIZATION AND CHILDREN

FIVE YEAR OLD THOMAS HAS ALWAYS BEEN CONSIDERED a shy child. Even as a toddler he remained very close to his mother and other adults in his life when placed in situations involving other children. In preschool, Thomas had a tendency to isolate himself and not interact with other children, which made his capacity to develop friends troublesome. He would often come home crying, saying that no one liked him and that he did not know what to say when other children asked him to play. This placed Thomas in a precarious position: on one hand he wanted to make friends, be like everyone else, and start to develop some cooperative friendships, but on the other his shyness and insecurity prevented him from being able to interact in successful ways.

The teachers at the preschool were also concerned. They felt that if Thomas did not start to develop some social skills soon his graduation into pre-kindergarten and kindergarten would be difficult for him, since social relationships are of primary importance in the grade school years.

At night Thomas would often have difficulty going to sleep, and in the morning he would resist going to school because he was afraid he would be lonely and not be able to find any friends. As he was beginning a school phobia condition, his parents decided they needed to help him learn to be more socially adept. To begin with, his mother asked if there were any children in his class whom he wished to become friends with. Thomas immediately responded that Brian, another five year old in his class, seemed like a boy who had a good heart. She then suggested he invite Brian to come over and have a play date in their house, and offered to help Thomas figure out things he could do with Brian that would make the play date successful and personally rewarding. When Thomas told his mother he wanted to enjoy playing games with his friends, she decided that before Brian came over, she would play their favorite family games with Thomas. While playing *Chutes and Ladders*, his mother first pretended as though she were a peer with whom Thomas could interact. This really helped Thomas see how to relate to someone. His mother realistically tried to play out what it might be like to play with other children. Later that day when Brian arrived, Thomas was noticeably less stressed. He immediately invited Brian to play games to which Brian agreed. Thomas felt so comfortable playing a few rounds of *Candy Land*, he actually asked Brian what he wanted to do, and Brian introduced him to playing *Hide and Seek*. Thomas was elated that he was finally learning how to make friends.

WHEN DOES SOCIALIZATION BEGIN?

The socialization of a child begins even before they are conceived. It is based upon the parental attitude regarding the importance they place on friendships, and the individual parent's experience and success in making and maintaining healthy friendships. The parent who places a high regard for the establishment of friendships tends to pass this trait down to their children; it manifests once they are at an age when they are functionally able to interact with their peers. Parental characteristics, including moral integration, fairness, compassion, sharing, comfort, and tolerance for social conflict, all actively contribute to how a child will approach social situations, and can predict how the child will interrelate with others. This is due to the fact that children internalize their parent's attitude in the early years of their development. Cliché as it is, children are sponges and will observe, accept, and adopt their parent's behaviors.

Although the parental attitude is a very important predictor of how successful a child will be in making and keeping friends, particular characteristics of the child will also influence how they will interact with another child.

Temperament: The inborn, constitutional, personality trait of the child is a very important predictor of the initial approach a child will utilize when addressing a potential new friend. For example, outgoing and spirited children tend to approach new social situations faster and with more ease than children who might be described as "slow to warm up" or shy. On the other side of the coin, children who might be described as temperamentally "strong-willed" or "stubborn" tend to have the most conflicts initially in their friendships due to their difficulty of tolerating frustration and disappointment.

Fine and Gross Motor Skills: Children who are comfortable with their bodies and who have a certain amount of physical ability to play with others tend to have an easier time making friends than children who are not as confident in this area.

Compassion: Compassionate children, or those who balance their personal needs with those of others, tend to be the most popular in the early years of friendship development. This is due to the fact that young children are accustomed to the love of a caring parent and will expect and be most familiar with peers who demonstrate similar traits.

Parents: Given that the establishment of friendships is one of the most important pillars of development and predictors of future success, parents who promote the establishment of friendship early on in their child's development help their children succeed long-term in this area. A parent can assist in the social development of their child by following some simple guidelines:

Play with your child. Parents who regularly play with their children from infancy onwards help them to internalize the importance of social relationships, and also help them learn how to understand and follow social rules. During the elementary school years, parents who take the time to play games and follow the rules also provide a foundation for how the child will conduct themselves when on their own with their peers.

Encourage play dates. The parent who is comfortable with their child separating from them and developing friends conveys to their son or daughter that it is okay to separate and become independently functional. Instinctively, children will worry that they are abandoning their mother or father if they wish to play with a peer and will subsequently refrain from asking for a play date due to this reason.

Assist in conflict resolution. When helping a child organize a play date, it is important the parent sets the rules with both children from the beginning of the date. Insisting on concepts such as sharing, taking turns, being considerate, and talking through conflicts provides the children with parental structure. Over time such concepts will be self-applied, but in the pre-school and early elementary school years, a helpful parent can really make a difference. When a conflict occurs during a play date, the observant parent should calmly help the children talk to one another and remain neutral while helping to identify and resolve the issue, simultaneously reassuring the children that conflict is normal amongst friends.

Gender differences and friendships. Although friendships are just as important for both girls and boys, each gender has different ways of interrelating with their peers at particular ages. For example, girls tend to be more verbal and creative, and boys tend to be more physical and competitive with their peers. It is more common for parents to have to break up interactions with a group of boys than girls through middle adolescence. Over time, however, the difference in play becomes more balanced, and usually by late adolescence children's friendships involve deep caring and sharing, utilizing both words and activities.

The establishment of friendships is essential for the normal development of a child. Friends developmentally supplement and sometimes replace parents as the child strives towards becoming an independent and autonomous individual. Friendships assist children in learning how to adapt to various situations and provide an outlet to discuss commonly shared experiences with someone who is going through similar developmental stages. Parents who understand the importance of these relationships and support their establishment assist their child with a very important aspect of their development.

Key Points:

1. **Parental friendships set an example for the socialization of the child.**
2. **Put children in positions where they can be successful based upon their developmental level.**
3. **Establishment of friends is essential to healthy development.**
4. **Friendships developmentally replace parents during times of child development.**
5. **Parents need to take a proactive role in creating and monitoring social situations.**

FAQ's

1. *What should I do if I have a good friend, but our young children do not socialize well together?*

The first step would be to try to get to the bottom of why they are they not connecting. Is it because their personalities are just too different? Is it something extraneous, for instance, something outside of their connection that is making them not get along, like not having any toys in common, or not having an adequate place to play? We want to find out the "why" first and try to fix this issue. If this step does not work and you really want your individual families to be friends, then the next effort would be a group event putting the two families together. Plan to do fun things which also create team building activities. For instance, you can play a game in which the two children are partnered against the parents. In effect they are forced to become allies, and oftentimes when there is a common goal or common activity the children become friends.

2. *How do I handle a child who likes to keep to himself in social settings with other children?*

First you need to assess whether this shyness is a personality variable. In essence, is this a temperamental/inborn quality of the child which is habitual and long lasting, or is it an internal conflict/neurotic conflict causing an inhibition? Perhaps the child is in a group which is too dissimilar to him. An example would be a girl who is a bit nerdy who wants to hang out with the popular girls, but doesn't have much to say because she is not like them and does not have the same interests as they do.

If you have a child who would rather be alone with his electronic games and computer instead of being with other children, there is something going on within that child. It is normal for children to want to socialize. If the child does not want to seek out connections with their peers it is an indication something developmentally and/or psychologically isn't where it ought to be. I would encourage parents to get to the bottom of this issue. There are two questions to ask: Is it historic, e.g. has it always been like this? Or has there been a trauma or did something happen that caused a regression whereby the child deterred from previously being sociable? For instance, if the child has just switched schools their behavior maybe reactive. If it is reactive, it is likely that the child will adjust over time when he/she adopts to the new school. On the other hand, if the avoidance of socialization is long-standing, the issues are deeper and you may need to get some help.

3. *What are common signs that my child is not developing well socially?*

- There is not an intrinsic drive to want to be social;

- They do not relate well to peers;
- They don't seem to have a sense of social appropriateness when they are within a peer group;
- They tend to be rejected by others (i.e. not invited to birthday parties; no invitations for play dates; there is not a reciprocal sense of people wanting to spend time with him/her);
- There is an over-dependency on parents which means the child remains predominantly attached to the parents, and bonds with parents instead of wanting to bond with friends. . We tend to see a gradual shift of children pushing away from or separating from their parents starting typically at 15–18 months of life. This is a wonderful developmental sign that they are growing up. How parents respond to their child's separation makes or breaks the psychological mind and development of the child.
- Social situations make the child anxious;
- The child does not like him/herself and assumes others will not like them either;
- They are not making any sort of attempt to fit in. For instance, they don't want to dress like others, see the same movies, or talk about the same video games.

CHAPTER 3

SAYING "NO" TO YOUR CHILDREN

SETTING LIMITS WITH YOUR CHILDREN IS ONE OF THE basic responsibilities of any parent, but also one of the most confrontational and difficult experiences. This is due to the fact that having to say "No" to a child inflicts discomfort and sometimes even pain, which goes against another basic parental responsibility, namely that of comforting and soothing a child. Such internal conflicts commonly create anxiety and at times these decisions, which are in the best interests of the child, may not be received as such. Most parents feel guilty when they have to frustrate their child or not provide them with the gratification which is assumed to bring joy and happiness to their child. Moreover, it is easier for child and parent alike to keep children happy by giving them what they want — at least in the short-term.

However, this is not the case when a child's desire for something does not reflect a healthy choice. Here the parent is placed in a challenging position: keep the child happy, or incur almost guaranteed disappointment and an unpleasant situation. Often, even though the parent is making the right decision, a child will express dismay through anger or sadness which makes the parent feel uncomfortable about having disappointed their child. For some parents, this experience is so upsetting that they give in to avoid having to deal with the alternative and allow their child to engage in activities which are not good for them. While this allows the parent to avoid feeling guilty or having to deal with an upset child, it does nothing but hurt the child's long-term ability to constructively deal with needs versus wants.

When 14 year old Samantha tried to convince her parents she could manage a co-ed pool party at their house on a Friday night without any parental supervision, her alligator tears made both of her parents go against their joint intuition that this was not a good idea. Sure enough, the party got out of hand and their neighbors ended up calling the police who found empty bottles of vodka all around the pool area and some very intoxicated teenagers. Samantha's parents felt awful. On the one hand they had wanted to please their daughter and truste her to be with her friends, but on the other hand, both parents intellectually knew it was not fair to place their young daughter in the role of policing her friends at a party.

Another obstacle preventing parents from saying "No" is their desire to be "liked" and not ignored by their child. Once children emerge from early childhood, most parents feel somewhat abandoned by their child as they strive towards independence and replace their parents with friends. This bewildering experience is painful for any parent. In the early years, our children can't get enough of us, but by the time they become teenagers, parents end up taking a number just to spend some quality time with them. Here, unconsciously, many parents will try to act "cool" in hopes their children will spend more time with them, be nicer to them, or even talk like a peer to them. The potential compromise, however, is that the parent is not looking out for possible hazards by not setting certain limits, or saying "No." Such was the case for 14 year old Nick whose father allowed him to occasionally drink a beer or two with him on the weekends thinking this experience would bring them closer and also take away Nick's curiosity to "experiment" with alcohol at parties. This effort backfired as Nick became the "experienced" drinker among his friends. His use of alcohol increased during high school which ended up hurting both his health and his grades.

While it always seems easier to gratify one's child wishes than frustrate them, the short-term gain can often lead to long-term problems. Saying "No" or frustrating one's child serves two purposes: first, it provides protection from potential negative events or influences, and second, it teaches children how to better tolerate frustration which is a vital life lesson, one that eventually becomes generalized to the outside world. Clearly, the hardest part of saying "No" to a child is how it makes a parent feel. Parents must understand that setting limits is another means of protection and love for their child. . In fact, when parents do say "No", the common result (after perhaps a temper tantrum or two) is a calming in the child's behavior and incurring a sense of respect for their parent.

Key Points:

1. **Parents often fear setting limits with their children because the parents want to be liked.**

2. **Saying "No" can make the parent feel guilty about causing sadness and pain in their child.**

3. **Setting appropriate limits for their child's development and safety are just as important as gratifying a child's wishes.**

4. **Once out of adolescence, the child often will thank their parent for being parental and watchful.**

FAQ's

1. *What if our child knows which parent is more lenient and uses this knowledge to their advantage?*

Then you have a smart child. They've figured it out and they will use this leverage as much as they can to their advantage. Just like everybody else, kids like to win — they don't like to lose. But if your child is polarizing one way or the other, (a) it is not good for them and (b) it is not good for you or your relationship with your spouse. It will cause something we call "splitting" which leads to all sorts of awful side effects such as animosity, anger, sadness, and despair. It is important parents work together collectively as a unit, which includes their expectations, requirements, manners, and accountability. There mustn't be a weak link or a strong link, but a parental link jointly emphasizing that "These are the important things" and that "We are here to make sure you do everything humanly possible to take care of yourself."

2. *What if Mom and Dad differ on their respective levels of strictness and punishment?*

Then you're normal in your relationship. The big question is how you can work together as a team to: 1) communicate the importance of certain requirements, and 2) insist on these conditions being met for the best interests of the child (which the child will not understand unless they are older and into adolescence).

It is very important that there isn't a good guy or bad guy, or a "Wait 'til your father gets home" type of environment fostered in your home. The children need to know their parents are invested in loving and protecting them and helping them develop into the best possible person they can be; that the parents are co-invested in making sure their child feels good about themself and strives as high as they can. Children should know and understand, habitually, that if they are not good bosses of their feelings, it is not that Dad or Mom will be mad at them, but that their parents worry about them and will do what it takes to make sure the children don't do the same thing again.

3. *How do you cope with/discipline a child who repeatedly does not accept "No" graciously?*

Pat yourself on the back! Your child has clearly identified themselves as being separate from you. However, if they continue to feel too separate from you, their behavior will get worse. They will continue to be unaccepting of the situation because they will feel completely entitled. This is because at this point they will have actually felt rejected by you.

So, to answer the question, you graciously accept the fact that "No" is an expected and necessary word for any developing child. The key is to understand this about your child and not attack their sense of independence and willful desires. Instead you need to help your child realize that sometimes we can get what we want and sometimes we can't, and that for the most part we get so much it usually equals out.

Conversely, the parent needs to understand the child's "No" and where it comes from, and not get angry at the child because they are telling you how they feel. If your child is repeatedly saying "No" to you it can be a sign they are trying to be independent, or it could be that there are things which are really upsetting them. In other words, are you saying "No" too much, so that they are getting mad? Do you ever say "Yes?" Do you help your children feel good when you say "Yes" so they recognize this pleasant feeling as well? It is a parent's job to discern if this behavior is a normal response in their child's development (they are being willful), or if there is more to it. Our job as parents is to be understanding and compassionate.

4. When is it okay for a parent to change their "No" to a "Yes"?

In very few circumstances does a parent fully believe a request is a clear cut "Yes" or a "No." A parent has to do their best to navigate between the two. A parent's desire to change "No" to a "Yes" is something that happens by the hour. There is frequently internal conflict whenever a parent has to agree or not agree to something. Keep the following in mind:

5. It is okay for a parent to change their answer when they have considered that the initial decision they made was not the best one based on new information;

It is okay to change their answer when the parent has thought it through from a realistic point of view and has decided to change their mind. If a parent changes their mind based on the fear of not being liked, or for some unrealistic reason, or as the result of a displaced reason such as being angry at a spouse, then changing the decision may not have been the best choice;

It is also okay to change their answer when the initial decision was not based on the actual circumstances, but instead was based on a progression of a generation, meaning it was based on the parent's own childhood and what they were or were not allowed to do as a child.

CHAPTER 4

SHOULD PARENTS LIE TO THEIR CHILDREN?

QUESTIONS, QUESTIONS, AND MORE QUESTIONS. From the moment our children start talking, the questions start rolling. At first, many questions are naive and are based on gathering understandable facts about the world. These are the easy "nuts and bolts" of helping children build their minds and are needed for optimal development. But even the answers to these types of questions need to be explained in ways in which your children can understand them; your answers must not be presented in ways that might cause them anxiety or overwhelm them. The key is to give our children only enough information to make them comfortable and not go beyond what they are able to digest as this might backfire and create panic.

As children grow their questions become much more personal about you, not as much as you as the adult, but you as a child and an adolescent. This is when it becomes very complicated. On the one hand, we want to teach our children to tell the truth, be honest, and have integrity. On the other hand, children use their parents as frames of reference and as their models for how to be now and how NOT to be, even when the adolescents are trying to differentiate themselves. Examples of complicated questions may have to do with study habits, grades, dating, sex, and the use of alcohol and drugs. Get ready, parents. If these questions have not reached your dinner table yet, they will. You had best be prepared for how you will respond. Think through your beliefs, hopefully based on optimizing your child's developmental, physical, and psychological well-being. Get ready for how to respond.

As children and adolescents, we all made our mistakes and hopefully learned from them. As parents, one of our basic jobs is to be the best teacher to our children as we can. Much of this is based on the mistakes we have made, what we have learned, and what we want to pass on. In many cases, parents have been very open with their children about the above types of questions (drugs, sex, alcohol, etc.), and feel as though they should be open with their children to "help" them avoid making "the same mistakes" they did as an adolescent. Unfortunately, the results of full disclosure tend to be very mixed and tend to be more negative than positive. If you are fortunate enough to have a very mature adolescent, they are less likely to call you a hypocrite when you tell them NOT to do something you did at their age. But remember, you are your child's model, and even though they may be trying to differentiate from you, they also often want to be like you — yes, they love and respect you and see you now as a healthy adult. You, therefore, are their window into the future, and they will internalize, "Well, my mom turned out okay and she used drugs when she was in high school."

The problem is that times have changed. The types and usage of drugs, teenage pregnancy, increased competition for getting into colleges, and much more has changed the world we experienced when we were in middle and high school. Our children need our protection now more than ever.

So, how can we be open and honest with our children without over-exposing them to information that may present us as being hypocritical? Considering the best interest of your child is the key here. We want our children to be healthy, confident, have solid self-esteem and friendships along with good grades, as they go through the difficult years of adolescence. As their parents, we are the gatekeepers and must present them with healthy choices irrespective of whatever mistakes we ourselves made in our earlier years. The answer is to keep the focus on them, not on us. A wonderful way to make a child or adolescent feel empowered when they ask you a good question is to tell them, "That is a great question you've asked me." But the answer you give must be based on two considerations: 1) the question they are asking is really about THEM, not you — it is a projection of their ideas; and 2) your job is to protect them. Therefore your answer is based on your knowledge as an adult, not as an adolescent!

The father of one of my patients told me how he tackled the sex question with his 14 year old son. When his son asked him when he first had sex, this father replied, "Great question and I am sure you are getting exposed to all sorts of influences and stories these days. What a tough place for you. I remember those days too. As your dad, I want you to come to me with these questions and I will help you sort through them." His son was persistent, "Dad, when did you have sex for the first time?" His father's wonderful response was, "It really doesn't matter what I may or may not have done, we are talking about you, and I am on your team. I do not feel as though adolescents should have sex until they are either at the end of high school or in college for a number of reasons." He then described the reasons to his son. Although he did NOT directly answer the question, he did not lie, but he did not disclose his own experience with sex for all of the reasons I have listed above. His son was a bit angry his dad did not discuss his history, but it's better to have your child or adolescent angry with you than engage them in a discussion that could harm them. We are all accustomed to our children feeling ambivalent towards us — this is all part of being a parent. There is no need to lie; just keep the focus on where it should be — on them, not you.

Key Points:

1. **Only give enough details to your child's questions to satisfy them.**
2. **Your children always identify with you and will repeat your patterns.**
3. **Too much personal disclosure causes more harm than good.**
4. **Always keep the best interest of your child in mind.**
5. **Keep the focus on them, NOT you — this is being honest and not lying.**
6. **Your job is to protect your child.**

FAQ's

1. *What is the appropriate age to have the "sex, drug, alcohol" talk with my child?*

It is appropriate anytime a child starts asking questions of their parents about any of these topics. But the parent must first take into consideration the age and developmental level of their child before determining how they will respond to the question. Irrespective of age, when a child comes to the parent and asks for information, it is essential that the parent give them information and lessen their potential anxiety or curiosity. One must be careful not to give too much information, or information that could inadvertently make the child more anxious. Proceed with caution. Commend them for bringing it up to you and tell them you are happy they asked your opinion, and that these are great questions. Encourage them to always come to you with any questions they have and assure them you will non-judgmentally respond to them.

2. *How important is it to dispel inaccuracies our child may be "learning" from his friends if we feel the topic itself is not yet age-appropriate?*

It is very important that parents understand that the peer environment is in direct competition with your family environment. If you do not respect your child's social and interpersonal world outside the family, you are setting yourself up for years of misery (which may even last longer than when they leave your house to go to college or to get married).

When you overhear information which comes your way from your child or their peer group acknowledge: 1) this is their world; 2) it is an important one; 3) any attempt to destroy it will only backfire. If, as a parent, you are hearing information you think is inaccurate and not age-appropriate, you are hearing it for a good reason. Your child would not be talking about it around you if they did not want you to know about it and need your help. So, don't blow it. Without humiliating your child in front of his peers, there is nothing wrong with making a comment to the effect that you respect everything you are hearing, but "One of the things I heard you say isn't exactly right."

3. *How do I get my child to talk with me about awkward topics?*

From a very early age you need to teach your child there is no such thing as an awkward topic, and that any topic will be viewed by you as normal and inquisitive. It is a good sign that your child is starting to ask questions and to question his/her world, self, and body. If awkward topics can be dispelled as being normal, and there are appropriate reality constraints placed on a child's thinking process, then topics don't become awkward; they become more necessary and they'll happen more often. Hopefully this interaction begins at an early age and lasts a lifetime. Any topic your child brings to you is not awkward — it's a good question.

CHAPTER 5

WHY HABITS ARE HARD TO BREAK

THIRTY-EIGHT YEAR OLD SARAH HAS DECIDED TO TRY to stop smoking for the fourth time this year, starting with her first attempt as one of her New Year's resolutions. In the past, she first attempted to stop "cold turkey" which did not work. Next she consulted with her personal physician and tried nicotine patches which lessened her desire to smoke, but she failed to fully comply with the prescription dosage and eventually gave up. Finally, last year, she tried hypnotherapy which worked for about a month. Sarah found her desire to smoke too strong to resist and returned to her two-pack-a-day habit. Recently, Sarah lost one of her maternal aunts to cancer, rejuvenating her desire to break her 15-year habit. Even though she intellectually understands the health risks, family history, and the likelihood of contracting cancer if she continues to smoke, her habit feels beyond her control and she is frightened that she will once again fail.

To make matters worse, Sarah's 14 year old daughter, Tiffany, has decided she wants to smoke also. Despite Sarah's objections when finding out that Tiffany wants to smoke, Sarah has been called hypocritical by her daughter who is stuck between trying to become her own person and at the same time identify with her own mother. This has caused extensive strife for Sarah because on the one hand she wants to give up her smoking habit, and on the other hand feels as though she can't and now her habit has trickled down to her daughter which is making her feel even more guilty about smoking. Additionally, Sarah has also been noticing that Tiffany has been stealing money out of her purse to buy cigarettes. This indicates to Sarah that her daughter may be developing both a psychological and chemical dependency on the same substance Sarah herself has been battling for over 15 years.

Sarah's story is an example of a common dilemma faced by many — bad habits which the individual consciously and intellectually understands are not in their best interest, but nevertheless the compulsion of the habit overrides good choices. Such habits are typically long-standing, often begin in adolescence, can affect other family members, and can last a lifetime.

In order to truly break a habit, we need to fully understand exactly what a habit represents. Habits are complex behaviors due to the fact that they are a part of our personality or character. The habit functions as an active component of a lifestyle serving a multitude of functions or needs. In other words, there are always two sides to a bad habit: one which is maladaptive, and the other serving some sort of "need." Professionally we call this aspect a "secondary gain" of the habit or symptom. Taken together, such an internal compromise or internal conflict explains why a bad habit is so difficult to conquer.

Giving up the symptom, or bad habit, constitutes a loss and often leaves the individual feeling vulnerable or anxious because the underlying conflict then becomes exposed and uncomfortable for the person. This dynamic helps to explain why oftentimes, as in the case of Sarah, the habit fails to extinguish itself. Although the person feels like a failure, another part of them feels protected. In addiction literature, another way of conceptualizing this aspect of the habit is referred to as the "psychological addiction." The underlying and typically unconscious aspect of the secondary gain is never uniform. Depending upon the personality of the person, such unconscious explanations could range from the desire to be taken care of to unconscious guilt with subsequent self-punishment, low self-esteem, and attention seeking, just to name a few. In order to fully conquer a bad habit, the individual must come to terms with this aspect of the habit in order to master its representation and eventually let it go, and perhaps find healthier ways of managing the anxiety. In many cases, psychotherapy is needed to determine this aspect of the habit and to assist the person in working through the process of change.

To further complicate matters, however, as in the case with smoking or drug usage, there is an additional component of a "physical addiction", where the body craves the substance when it becomes absent. This is often why breaking a substance habit requires medical consultation in order to advise the patient how to slowly wean the body off the addiction.

In Sarah's case, she decided to begin psychotherapy in order to help her find the underlying causes of her smoking habit. This decision was based on her fear of following in her aunt's early demise if she did not change this aspect of her personality. While this example illustrates how oftentimes it takes a family or personal crisis to motivate someone to change a bad habit, this does not have to be the case in every situation. Most people can change even the worst of habits if they invest themselves in seeking both understanding and following through with a healthy plan.

Key Points:

1. **Bad habits are woven into our personality.**
2. **Secondary gains keep the habit going even if it's maladaptive.**
3. **Understanding the function of the habit is essential to breaking it.**
4. **The longer you've had the habit, the harder it is to break.**
5. **The anxiety behind the habit needs to be managed healthfully.**
6. **Parents need to help children break bad habits.**
7. **Psychotherapy can be very helpful in developing insight and planning change.**

FAQ's

1. How do I know if my bad habit goes beyond a physical addiction?

If all measures have been taken medically to deplete or alleviate the physical piece of addiction, and the person continues to crave or feel as though they cannot survive without whatever they are addicted to, this would constitute what we have referred to as a psychological addiction. It would need to be investigated and worked through in order for the addiction to come to an end.

In the case of 32 year old Sarah, she might go to her internist and tell him she wishes to break her smoking habit whereby she is prescribed a therapeutic regimen of nicotine replacement. Despite all medical tests indicating the nicotine is no longer causing Sarah to want to go back to smoking, further investigation needs to be made into why she continues to want to smoke when it appears to her as only a physical addiction.

2. *What are the warning signs of a bad habit?*

- An unrealistic sense that we cannot live without feeling irrationally connected to the habit;
- Interpersonal, occupational, developmental and even physical negative consequences as a result of the focus on the agent of the habit;
- The focus on "bad," as in a bad habit also speaks to possible masochistic or self-sabotaging dynamics, even though the person might consciously acknowledge the habit is unhealthy and harmful for them despite a continual investment in doing something self-destructive.

3. *What is the difference between a bad habit and a vice?*

A vice can have normal or abnormal properties. Normal properties are when a person likes to do something on occasion because it makes them feel good or brings them some happiness, and when the activity doesn't negatively impact the ongoing routine of their successful life. Then a vice is not considered a bad habit.

An example would be 26 year old Tom, a recent architectural school graduate, who loves to gamble. In fact, he takes trips every two months to Las Vegas just to satisfy his vice. However, Tom only brings $500 with him, because despite his love of gambling, he is smart enough to realize the odds are always with the house. He acknowledges that even though he may win sometimes, he could lose his shirt if he lets his gambling love turn into a bad habit. Interestingly, Tom is ahead of the game; he has been winning more than he has been losing, and he knows things can change. Therefore he is in control of his vice.

CHAPTER 6

WHY MOMS GET DUMPED BY THEIR CHILDREN

DEBBIE ALWAYS THOUGHT SHE HAD A GREAT RELATIONSHIP with her two and a half year old son, Benjamin. As a full-time stay-at-home mom during his infancy, she and Ben were close and happy as the two of them spent hours of time daily bonding, learning, and playing. It was during his third year, however, that their relationship went through a significant change. Benjamin frequently became frustrated with Debbie whenever she would say "No" to him or not gratify his numerous wishes. As he was becoming more verbal, he would let her know his dismay by telling her he "did not like her", that she "was a bad mom" and he would often pout and ignore her. This left Debbie feeling both bewildered and sad, questioning, "How could he change so quickly?" and "Where did I go wrong developing a rude child?"

Little did Debbie realize that what Benjamin was doing was a very good sign of normal development. Between the second and fourth years of life, as children become more comfortable with themselves (usually due to good parenting), they desire more independence. They try to find ways to separate from their parents, especially their mother. Despite a strong need to remain close to their primary caregivers, another part of the child has identified that they are a separate being and they want to explore their world with more autonomy. The mother, therefore, becomes the obstacle to such intentions and is targeted as the enemy. This is balanced, however, with the child's continued need to be nurtured and to retain the love and admiration of the parent.

A healthy conclusion to the "terrible twos" is usually marked by the child feeling internally loved as an individual and also learning to comply with certain rules that Mom and Dad insist upon being followed. The early childhood years between ages five and six are less argumentative; the child is practicing being a "big girl" or a "big boy" and tries to relate on a more mature level with his or her parents. Fantasies of being adults, superheroes, princesses, and policemen occupy hours of imaginative play and can be very entertaining for the parents. However, once the child learns more about the realities of life and that their wishful magical desires are impossible, they become disappointed and frustrated. Such feelings then become misplaced onto the parents, especially the mother, and once again requests for compliance are often met with resistance and anger. As a result of their grander disappointments, everything the parent directs them to do becomes "unfair" and simple requests from taking a shower to completing homework spark disproportionate levels of defiance. Arguments become common. Once again, the mother is the "bad news" messenger and gets an earful.

Sometimes the years between ages 10 and 11 are calmer, depending upon the temperament of the child and how well he or she manages feelings of anger and frustration. As pre-adolescence and the adolescent years run their course, Mom once again becomes a frequent target of displeasure. For the girls, the cause is a combination of envy, competition, and wishes for more independence. For the boys, it is a combination of identifying Mom as both powerful and also a member of the opposite sex, causing anxiety and, at times, significant distance between mother and son. Once adolescence is over, however, both boys and girls typically develop healthy relationships with both of their parents. They have worked through the kinks of development and are, once and for all, confident independent beings.

To make matters even more complicated, fathers tend not to receive the extent of the negativity the mother endures. This is due to the fact that fathers tend to be more of a medium between mother and child and assist in the process of separation. The mother is viewed as the one who is the primary rules setter and arbiter, and therefore receives the brunt of the child's negativity.

So, how can mothers weather the storms of their children's need to separate from them while continuing to love, nurture and parent them through this process? The mothers who understand and practice the important principles written below tend to optimally manage these stages with their children. Their child moves through his or her development with less difficulty then when mothers and fathers react in ways which make their child feel either bad or abandoned.

Key Points:

1. **Understand that maternal rejection is a normal and expected aspect of development.**
2. **Don't take it personally.**
3. **Manage your feelings of sadness and frustration.**
4. **Continue to be loving and empathic, but set limits when the negativism crosses the line.**

5. **Get your spouse to support your position.**
6. **Realize that these are only stages.**

FAQ's

1. ***What steps can the secondary caregiver (often the father) take during this time to lessen the burden or bridge the gap between child and mother?***

Realize what's happening and understand that both child and wife are going through developmental change; that with any change comes anxiety and sadness, as well as excitement. In the position of father, the task is to mediate by being able to support the feelings and needs of his wife while at the same time understand the psychological and developmental needs of his child. The father can then take this important information and use it to comfort his wife and his child to make the developmental shifts go more smoothly than otherwise expected.

2. ***How should mothers address this issue with their children?***

They should *not* address this with their children because it is not an issue — it is a reality. When children separate from their parents, it is a healthy step towards individuation and self-comfort. To do this, children have to feel they can replace within themselves everything their parents have taught them. Their own struggles with separation cannot communicate these feelings; instead a child often rejects them as a way to indicate respect and acknowledgment about a sense of being able to be independent from their parents. Parents need to know, mothers especially, that in order to separate and individualize, children need to take their parents off a pedestal in order to understand (with the continued assistance of parents) that they can stand on their own two feet.

If mothers do not understand the normalcy of this and don't pat themselves on the back when their child wants to separate from them after early years of one-ship, the child will suffer. In other words, moms need to manage their feelings of sadness about their child growing up. They need to enjoy the benefits of watching their children strive independently and make good choices, instead of becoming angry and despondent about their child's growth.

If, however, the child's manner and behavior during this process of "dumping" their mothers is deemed inappropriate, then both parents need to first validate the child's feelings of irritation, anger, and frustration, but make sure the child conveys their feelings in ways which don't make matters worse. As I often say, "Use **your** words" when instructing children to express their feelings. You may have to encourage them to use different words. Accept it, don't take it personally, remaining connected, interested, and in love with your children — that needs to stay fixed.

Mothers should not be talking to their child saying, "Oh, you are growing up and you don't need me as much," because this will make children feel afraid. Parents are always on call 24/7 for their children from infants to adults; they should be as tuned in as much as they can to who their children are and how they are feeling. When things happen, the parent has to try to understand the situation. If the child takes it too far it is okay to say, "Look, I know you get mad at me whenever I tell you that you cannot stay out after midnight, but you cannot call me a b-tch." The parent needs to set boundaries; don't punish the feelings, but help the child manage the internalization and the expression of the same. Children act out when they are uncomfortable. When children are good bosses of their feelings, they do not act out because it is contained; they know how they feel, they process through it, and they come up with other ways to modulate it.

3. How should mothers adjust their expectations/interaction with their child to make this developmental period smoother for everyone?

Know what you are in store for ahead of time. Parents need to be educated and mothers need to know there will be ebbs and flows, ups and downs. There will be times when their services are essential and other times when they will be obsolete, but they will always be looked to for comfort and help.

Know what is coming up. Know there will be three primary developmental periods where children push away from their parents: toddler-hood, middle childhood, and adolescence. During those periods parents are de-idealized, especially the mother, but in adolescence this occurrence is equally shared. If you think your husband is getting off the hook with your nine year old, just wait until he is 13 or 14. Then the father will bear the brunt of the adolescent's behavior and most likely have it even worse than the mother as he says "No" to the child's demands.

CHAPTER 7

RAISING CHILDREN'S SELF-ESTEEM

NINE YEAR OLD DAVID IS THE YOUNGEST OF THREE boys; one brother is 16 and the other is 12. Both are gifted athletes and do very well in school. To intensify such talents, both brothers brag about their accomplishments to David who has been diagnosed with some learning differences, and is small and physically immature for his age. Like most nine year olds, David compares himself to his siblings and his parents who are also successful in their own traits. Because of these external influences, David puts his heart and soul into everything he takes on whether it is sports or school. He feels he comes up short; as hard as he tries, he never seems to achieve the same level of success as his siblings and parents. This has caused significant stress and concern for David as he worries his family will lose confidence and respect for him if he is not as good as they are. What is missing here is David's sense of himself and the recognition of his own talents, independent of those of others. In fact, unlike most nine years olds, he seldom brags about his accomplishments which he does have in other areas of his life such as in music and art. But because of shortcomings in his mind when he compares himself to the rest of his siblings, he feels damaged and inadequate. He will frequently call himself names and tell people he doesn't want to try new things because he is afraid he will not be good at them.

Most recently David has been calling himself stupid and dumb. Such internal statements have caused him to socially pull away from many of his friends whom he also views as more successful. Despite the fact that David has his own talents, he doesn't recognize them based on internal expectations that he has to be good at all these other things in which his family excels.

Over the past four decades, a variety of different theories have been introduced to explain how a child develops self-esteem. In the 1960s and 1970s, emphasis was placed on compliance and adherence to societal rules and fulfillment of external expectations leading to optimal feelings of self-efficacy. In the 1980s, more emphasis was placed on individual differences and personal creativity as the determining factors underlying positive self-regard. In the 1990s and leading into the millennium, there has been an even greater shift towards the importance of the individual above and beyond external criteria. Some theorists have proposed this has actually caused a trend towards increased narcissism, disrespect for authority, and future disappointment in reference to relationships and occupational satisfaction, eventually leading to an overall decrease in the level of self-esteem. This recent trend could explain why general statistics of depression in children, adolescents, and young adults has risen over the past ten years. This new *Generation Me*, as recently explored in a book of the same title by San Diego State University's Jean M. Twenge, Ph.D., offers caution towards the way society presently believes self-esteem is derived.

Self-esteem is defined by the personal perception one has of themself as he or she experiences personal success combined with the appraisal of others and society. In other words, it is derived from a combination of both internal and external validation. Over the past 15 years or so, there has been less emphasis on the importance of external validation, and an increase in one's personal impressions of themselves irrespective of outside evaluation. This, according to Dr. Twenge, is dangerous, because it leads to a coupling of potential false expectations and a general disrespect for external criteria and validation. The eventual outcome of this trend could be a lack of accountability for one's personal shortcomings with blame for lack of success being misdirected upon external causes.

Taken together, the underpinnings of self-esteem need to be revisited. Whereas the trends have been from one extreme to the other, i.e. adherence to outside requirements/standards versus personal belief in self, an appropriate combination of the two approaches need to be emphasized. If children and adolescents are held accountable to various common standards such as respect, personal responsibility, good morals, and achievement necessities, reaching these levels will give them a sense of success and confidence which will lead to enhanced self-esteem. This becomes actualized when their success brings them certain rewards, such as praise from parents, social acceptance, good grades, or admission to college. If these ideals can be combined with an emphasis on personal uniqueness and individual difference then the child will also derive esteem from not only fulfilling important external criteria, but also from seeing themselves as a unique individual with special talents. This combination blends the benefits of varying trends over the past 40 years and leads to optimal self-esteem in children.

Key Points:

1. **Emphasize the importance of adherence to societal standards.**
2. **Support and award compliance with success-based activities.**
3. **Emphasize personal responsibility for actions.**
4. **Reinforce individual achievement and talents.**

FAQ's

1. *How can parents begin to instill values of high self-esteem in very young children?*

It's always important for parents to help their children establish realistic and good feelings about themselves. Even as little children, once they can comprehend self-awareness, it is important that parents help children feel positive about their minds, bodies, and activities by pointing out to them how good it feels when they achieve something. For instance, four year old Billy loves to show his muscles off to his mother; in fact, he asks her to squeeze his biceps. When he flexes for her, his mother smiles and responds, "Wow, you are getting so strong and so big! That must feel wonderful to you." Her son's smile couldn't be any bigger as he gives his mother an equally big hug. Mom has attuned herself to the importance of how that flexing must have felt to him, a pride even Billy wasn't fully aware of.

2. *How can parents help children address disappointments/rejections that hurt their child's self-esteem?*

Help them understand that disappointments, misgivings, rejections and losses, despite feeling really bad, happen sometimes and it is not the end of the world; that many good things happen also. In fact, when most people take good care of themselves and are nice to other people, they tend to be the least disappointed with themselves. Disappointing or rejecting moments, unless they happen too frequently, should not seriously affect the child's self-esteem. In most cases the child's life is balanced between successful, joyful, happy moments, and the frustrating, difficult, and sometimes even traumatizing moments they have to withstand. But if the child's ego is healthy, then a disappointing moment doesn't last longer than one would expect.

3. *What are the signs that my child's high self-esteem is becoming over-confidence?*

A key sign is when your child starts to brag in public. Despite the importance of a child's self-bragging and equally important bragging to one's parents, this sign of self-confidence should initially be met with excitement for how your child is feeling. If such robust feelings become unmanageable and infiltrate into their peer group, school ground, baseball team, scouting group, etc., then your child needs some help in containing their good feelings. On the other hand, sometimes children might express a sense of over-confidence as a way of compensating for actually not feeling so assured. Once again, the parent needs to be a good detective in trying to determine if an observance of over-confidence is a leaking of healthy self-esteem, or a consequence of a cry for help from the child. In other words, a child who is appearing overly confident, but is actually insecure, may be telling the parent they need more help to feel better about themselves.

CHAPTER 8

WARNING SIGNS

FOR THE LAST SIX MONTHS ALL HELL HAS BROKEN LOOSE in the Smith family. Thirteen year old Karen, who had previously done extremely well in grade school, has now begun middle school and her grades have fallen as well as her personal care and the quality of friends she has decided to make. At first her parents thought it was some sort of an adjustment to a new school and new friends, and the fact that many of her friends from grade school had gone off to different schools. However, as Karen's mother would tidy up Karen's room, she started to notice things that made her concerned. On the corner of her desk she found what appeared to be a marijuana pipe. This caused tremendous anxiety for Karen's mother, as her brother was a habitual drug user throughout middle and high school. She had the sinking feeling in her stomach that her daughter was going to follow the same path as Karen's brother.

However, due to a desire not to accept it, Karen's mother did not address the pipe with Karen; she hoped this was a one-time event or maybe not Karen's pipe at all, but that of one of her friends. But the next week Karen's mother found two empty beer cans in her trash can underneath some paper. As she looked more closely at the cans she noticed a message on the side of one beer can saying, "You're so cool Karen." This confirmed that her daughter was obviously using alcohol and marijuana at least sparingly. At this point Karen's mother felt she could not hide her findings any longer. In some way finding the paraphernalia was a cry for help from her daughter as she wasn't managing things for herself in a healthy manner.

After the beer can incident Karen's mother discussed the situation with Karen's father. The two of them decided to sit down with Karen and disclose to her what they had found, and mandate that Karen talk to somebody to get to the bottom of why she decided to start using alcohol and drugs when she started middle school.

Dangerous games, failing grades, drug and alcohol abuse, habitual rebellious behavior, and in the worst case, teenage suicide attempts, are all examples of "warning signs" that a "tween" or adolescent is in trouble; that their behavior is not normal as compared to what is considered expected behavior for a teenager. The old adage that "kids will be kids" can be a dangerous assumption if one does not fully understand what is considered "normal" versus abnormal behavior when parenting a middle or high school-aged boy or girl. As psychologists, psychiatrists, and psychoanalysts, we speak of the typical processes of separation and individuation as children and adolescents alike consciously and unconsciously attempt to separate themselves and become psychologically independent from their adult counterparts. They act and do things differently in efforts to feel less dependent and more grown up. But parents must observe and address the path their child chooses based on both the personality and particular conflicts each child and adolescent endures.

Another important consideration is that by definition, adolescents tend to feel normally invincible, and their judgment tends to be commonly inconsistent based on the influences of strong feelings of aggression and sexuality which put great stress on their conscience. Coupled with peer influences, pressure to do well in school, and a more or less self-centered view of the world due to their general sense of vulnerability, decisions are often half thought through and mistakes happen from time to time. When this occurs, most "good" parents set limits and the behaviors calm down, until the next period of "not thinking" happens. However, occasional poor judgment is far different than consistent investments in self-compromising behaviors which tend to place this group of children into frequent states of peril. We see these choices as symptoms of something much larger going on inside the adolescent, causing disturbance and subsequent maladaptive behaviors.

Exactly what is going on inside of the particular child needs more investigation to determine whether or not they are depressed, simply going through a rough developmental period, or withstanding an even more debilitating personality disturbance. It takes an invested parent who is observing their child on a daily basis and who has some sense of what is considered normal or not, to make the determination as to whether or not their child needs help.

In most cases, when parents find their child is going down a less than optimal pathway, they intervene and talk with them. If there is a lack of change, the parents seek professional help for their child. This is why most adolescents are neither depressed nor failing out of high school. Parents need to be constantly alert to how their child is managing his or her life during these critical years. We all know that most adolescents do not talk openly to their parents, but their behavior usually speaks loud and clear as to how they are really feeling about life. Very few children who are really suffering lack easily observable symptoms.

Key Points:

1. Immediate, calm, and attentive action by parents is the best response to any warning signs.
2. When parents intervene, their goal should be to eliminate or decrease symptoms while simultaneously addressing the root problem.
3. Symptoms are basically anything that is evidence of conduct which is self-compromising to a child or adolescent, but the top most common signs are as follows:
   - Failing grades in school;
   - Habitual risk-taking behaviors;
   - Daily negative self-statements;
   - An absence of friendships;
   - Evidence of self-injurious activities (i.e. cutting);
   - Poor hygiene after age 12;
   - School behavior problems;
   - Trouble with the law;
   - Consistent oppositional attitude towards all adults;
   - Evidence of drug and alcohol paraphernalia.

FAQ's

1. *How do I figure out what is at the root of my child's warning signs/ symptoms?*

It is hard, as a parent, to get to the root of the matter because you are in it, you are a part of it, and you are not an objective party. You are not someone who can stand outside and say, "Okay, what's going on in my child's head and life that is causing him to be distressed?" because you might be part of the puzzle. It is always beneficial to get an outside person to help you assess both the severity of the warning signs and to determine the root so the behavior doesn't continue. As a parent you are in a position to be able to identify the warning signs, be compassionate and supportive, and try to work together with your child to discern what this might be about. But if the warning signs are indeed severe enough, get outside help to make sure you are not missing something you might be actively a part of and biased about because you are in it with them.

2. *How do I intervene without pushing my child further away?*

Start out by telling your child you respect their point of view, their life, their friendships, and who they are. Because of your commitment and job as a parent, by default or definition you are concerned when something comes up that could directly or indirectly affect their health or well-being. Ask if there is something you need to talk to them about. Tell them you are doing this not because you hate them, but because you care about them, then express what your concerns are about what it is that has happened. Depending on their answer and whether or not they seem to be amiable about what you have to say, take everything into consideration. If necessary, you leave it be, but if they continue to do something you truly believe is going to substantially affect their life, you may have to play your parent trump card. This means telling them they will not like it, but it will have to be okay.

3. What are common toddler-age warning signs that may lead to more serious problems in the future?

Serious disturbances typically root and gain their building blocks within the first three years of life. There are some patterns which may lead to serious problems if they are not handled well, such as:

- An inability to comfortably want to be separate from Mom and Dad;
- Inability to sleep in their own bed;
- Temper tantrums so severe that nothing seems to soothe them and they interfere more than would be expected of a normal toddler;
- An absence of what is known as parallel play and desire for socialization;
- An inability to tolerate the absence of a parent when they are not in direct sight (serious separation anxiety);
- Any overt symptoms such as head banging, incessant rocking;
- Inability to form interpersonal attachments;
- Any self-injurious or other-injurious activities;
- Despite toddler age being a time for toilet training, problems can arise when a child withholds their bowels to a point of physical pain.

CHAPTER 9

THE SIGNIFICANCE OF PLAY

THREE YEAR OLD BRIAN WAS PLAYING WITH HIS OLDER sister's playhouse on the weekend prior to beginning his first day of preschool. His play consisted of having a girl doll get out of her bed, walk down the stairs, eat breakfast, and join the mother doll as they walked out of the house into a toy Barbie jeep. The jeep drove off to another location, which happened to be a desk chair designated as a supermarket. As they departed the car, Brian sent each figure to different locations throughout the market and assigned each of them different tasks. Each minute or so, however, he had the little girl visit her mother as they passed each other in the market. As they would pass, the girl doll would say, "Hi Mommy" and then continue to complete her tasks. After a few minutes, Brian loaded both figures back into the jeep and returned them home. He seemed happy they had completed the shopping journey and were once again reunited.

Given the timing of Brian beginning preschool the following Monday, this play example indicated Brian's attempt to become comfortable with having to separate from his mother. This form of practicing is a very adaptive way in which children prepare themselves for new adventures. In Brian's case, he was testing out his independence while checking to be certain his mother was close by just in case there was a problem. The joy at the end of the story indicates Brian's comfort with being able to "shop" on his own and then return to the safety of his home. His changing of his gender to a girl was an attempt to further manage his anxiety about separating from his mother.

"Play" serves to enhance development, allowing for internal thoughts, feelings, and concerns to be manifested in a safe and creative environment. For most children, play is a central way to convey how they feel and think rather than through the use of words. The process of playing helps to decrease anxiety and bolster confidence by allowing the child to practice new concepts and prepare for new experiences. In addition, play also helps to test out hypotheses, learn new rules, and conquer inhibition. Depending upon the age of the child, play will represent different developmental milestones. For example, in Brian's case, he was testing the concepts of object permanence and object constancy, both age-appropriate. Here, up to the age of five, most children have difficulty with the concept of irreversibility and struggle to believe that what was once lost can be found. This developmental reality underlies the common separation anxiety most parents experience when they first drop off their children to preschool and even through kindergarten. When children master this cognitive acquisition, the anxiety subsides, and they are no longer afraid to be apart from their parents for short periods of time.

In middle to late childhood (ages 6 to 11), play changes from a fantasy level to one involving more cooperation and adherence to rules. This transition runs in conjunction with changes in cognitive processing and moral reasoning. Common to this period are board and sport games where the children become obsessed with rules and what is considered right versus wrong. As children of this age play together, rule usage becomes more integrated and they learn to better cooperate and manage feelings of losing. Adolescent play involves sports, creative activities, and intensified socialization, such as small group activities, dances, and other types of outings.

Play should also continue throughout adulthood. Adult play serves as a stress release, a means of social interaction, and as a method of sharing and communicating with peers. In fact, adults who have a healthy "play life" tend to be happier and live longer. At each developmental level, it is important that the toys and the style/game of play are age-appropriate so the individual can utilize their creativity to its full extent.

Key Points:

1. **Play assists in the development of the mind.**
2. **Play is a window into the world of the child's mind.**
3. **Play assists in emotional development and self-regulation.**
4. **Children who play have fewer problems with aggression.**
5. **Play characteristics change over time.**
6. **Play materials must be age-appropriate and plentiful to avoid boredom.**
7. **Play should continue throughout adulthood.**

FAQ's

1. *What are the signs of age-inappropriate play?*

This could be one of two extremes; either the child is not playing thematically, or with objects that would be expected in the particular age group. An example of age appropriate play would be a seven year old who is still living in a predominantly fantasy world and playing with fantasy objects. On the other hand, inappropriate play would be a child who is playing with things that are too mature for his or her age. For example, a five year old playing with guns which can shoot something could cause over-stimulation and even injury to the child.

2. *When is "play" too much like reality?*

To begin with, if the play entails the possibility that someone could actually get hurt then it is too much. If the play gets carried away to the point where it can cause problems for parents, the child or another child, it is too much. Also, if the play isn't play anymore and becomes an action, this can be a problem. For instance, we hear the stories of children watching too much violence on television and the violence then trickles onto the playground. Or your child is playing a video game and it is inappropriate for his age, such as a five year old playing *Call of Duty* or *Grand Theft Auto.* . Because the content of these games is too mature for the child, he becomes anxious and overwhelmed, and might act out in reality what he now perceives to be reality.

3. *Should parents seek to participate in and play down to the level of the game/role play with their children?*

Parents should always to try to play with their child if the child invites and welcomes their participation. If a parent thinks something being enacted in a game is too much, inappropriate for the child, or damaging to the child, the adult can be clever in trying to, within the scene, illustrate how the child's actions might have a negative impact on them or another child. In a nice way and in an indirect fashion, the parent can teach the child about cause and effect.

CHAPTER 10

TRANSITIONAL OBJECTS

EVER WONDER WHY YOUNG CHILDREN BOND TO CERTAIN objects within their second year of life? Most parents share stories of their children having a favorite blanket, stuffed animal, or even a piece of clothing which the child carries with him or her on a daily basis, to and from places both inside and outside of the house. In fact, many children hold onto such objects well into their adulthood and revert back to them at particular times in their lives. This was the case with 17 year old Joni when she was packing her suitcases to leave for college. She insisted her mother find "Fluffy", the cherished stuffed cat she'd been attached to from ages two through six, because she "must" take "Fluffy" to college with her! Her mother concluded that "Fluffy" most likely disintegrated from significant use, but creatively found the same exact stuffed animal on eBay and sent it along with Joni to Stanford. Joni was relieved, yet a bit disappointed it was not the "exact Fluffy." Nevertheless, this one did the trick.

In other cases, children incorporate bonding objects into things like quilts, clothing, and other more mature articles. Here the impact of the transitional object continues to provide the individual with a reference to the past throughout their lives. So, what is this all about and why are such items so important for most children? The bonding to a transitional object usually develops as the toddler is attempting to comfortably separate from their primary caregiver, which is usually the mother. Children face the conflict of wanting continued attentive nurturing to help them manage stress, while another part of them desires autonomy. As a result, the young child searches for a compromise. Here the all-important transitional object becomes a symbol of the process. The object, in the magical mind of the toddler, carries the same comfort, solitude, soothing, and emotional support as did that early caretaker, but gives the toddler control of when and where it is utilized. If you watch a toddler with his or her transitional object, it is usually activated during times of transition or anxiety. Frequently, for example, the transitional object is taken to bed at night, to preschool, and often on vacations or other activities which are novel and tenuous. The function of this object is to provide comfort and assurance. The "Fluffy" carries almost the same power as the loving mother and father who took away stressful feelings from inside the young child; it makes them feel safe and content.

Usually, over time, the transitional object loses its magical power and is no longer needed as the child is able to internalize the important functions from their parents and the projected qualities of the transitional object. Optimally, the child becomes able to self-soothe in times of stress. This then leads to a sense of confidence and self-esteem.

However, the need for a loving parent and a transitional object will resurface in the lives of both children and adolescents as they withstand the throes of growth, change, stress, and development. Periodically, throughout the lives of school age children all the way through high school adolescence, times for that loving parent/object crutch will be necessary and are normal. For some, the parent is the sought after comfort source, and for others it may be that special early teddy bear or blanket that the child held on to during times of fear and agony.

Unlike the necessity for a child to wean from breast feeding, bottle feeding, pacifiers, and diapers, the transitional object is timeless. In other words, the transitional object is not much different psychologically from a child and adolescent occasionally needing their mom or dad to help them through a difficult time. Perhaps if transitional objects were encouraged early in a child's life, the need for pathological external conditions for relief from stress later in life, such as alcohol and drug usage, would not be as prevalent.

Key Points:

1. **Introduce transitional objects early in a child's life.**
2. **Once obtained, buy a supply of the same object in case it is lost.**
3. **Never take it away.**
4. **During times of distress, encourage the use of the object for comfort.**

FAQ's

1. *What are warning signs that a child's transitional object is too much of a crutch?*

A transition object should never be seen as a crutch, but rather as something helpful. In fact, the advent of a transition object is to give the child something in place of their mother to help with the separation and individuation process. Many children keep their transitional objects even as far as college because it is something that can be used to help soothe one's self in times of dismay. If the transitional object in some way or form prevents the child or adolescent from developing healthy interpersonal relationships, then the object could be considered a crutch. But in all likelihood, the real crutch is the reason behind why the child is continuing to hold on to the object. If that is dealt with the child will give up the object.

2. *Should we try to introduce a transitional object or wait for our child to choose one?*

Parents can introduce an array of objects to a child in infancy to help the child with the process of healthfully separating from them. Transitional objects can be anything from a stuffed animal, a blanket, to a piece of clothing — it does not really matter. Allowing the child to choose from a variety of things is always a good idea.

3. *Should the lack of a transitional object be worrisome in my child's development?*

Not necessarily. Not all children develop transitional objects. In extreme cases the inability to bond with a transitional object could be a sign of a pervasive developmental disorder such as autism. This would only be shown to be correct if, aside from the child not bonding to a transitional object, they were also not bonding to other people. But most children will either develop a transitional object or it will be the parent, until hopefully the child will give up the object for something like a sport, or someone else like a girlfriend or boyfriend.

CHAPTER 11

THE DAD TOY

ANY INVESTED FATHER REALIZES THE SAME PHENOMENON: once their child turns approximately four years of age, Dad becomes their child's favorite "toy" and the child seems to never get enough of him until they turn approximately ten years of age. While on a family vacation, my three children decided to altogether bypass the entire children's program on a Princess Cruise in exchange for me playing the role of their 24/7 entertainer, playmate, coach, and teacher. They explained to me I was "more fun" than any child's program, and that all they wanted to do for seven days was hang out with me. So, after about 30 games of shuffleboard, 25 games of ping pong, 7 or 8 visits to the arcade, hours of swimming every day, various board and electronic games, storytelling, reading, and much more, the cruise was over and school and work resumed. My kids expressed that it was one of the best trips ever. During the trip, I also spoke with other "dad toys" and found similar experiences from them as well. Together we concluded it was a wonderful, albeit at times tiring, experience. All concluded that the observed benefits in our children were well worth it. We commonly observed there was less acting-out, a greater interest in learning, more demonstrative levels of self-confidence, and an increased sense of independence. One father I spoke with who had been retired for the past two years told me that the hardest part of his returning to do some consulting work was the effect it was going to have on his sons. They had enjoyed in his attention and were saddened by the impending change.

Such real-life experiences support the research on the multitude of benefits associated with fathers who play with their children. Due to the differences in the way fathers play as compared to mothers (namely dads tend to be more physical and utilize friendly competition), such interaction correlates to greater self-esteem, easier experiences with separation from the mother, greater assertiveness, and a heightened desire to learn new tasks.

In contrast, before the age of three or four, most children prefer playing and bonding with their mothers due to the fact that they have been the primary object in the life of the infant and toddler. But as the young child becomes more comfortable with him or herself, they desire more independence and are able to break away from their mothers. This is the time when fathers become popular and essential in the process. Unfortunately, some fathers experience "rejection" from their young infant and toddler and then resist the new opportunity to get involved when the time is right. It is very important that fathers understand how development unfolds in the lives of their children so they do not feel left out or unimportant. The truth is, after the age of three or four, the impact of the father's influence remains essential throughout all of childhood and adolescence, which can be very rewarding if the father avails himself of the opportunity. The "dad toy" becomes a child's favorite pastime if made available and plentiful, especially between the ages of 3 and 10. No need for trips to toy stores and amusement parks — just get out there and play with your children.

Key Points:

1. **Fathers are the child's favorite toy from ages 3 to 10.**
2. **The benefits of "dad play" are numerous in the development of children.**
3. **Make weekly "alone" dad time available to your children.**
4. **Enjoy it while it lasts! Once he or she becomes a teenager, friends will replace you!**

FAQ's

1. *Your "vacation" left little time for Dad to get a break. How do you afford yourself personal time without neglecting your child's thirst for the "dad toy?"*

Balance your day for alone time. It is important for dads and moms on any vacation to have some down time. Otherwise, if you don't refuel yourself you will not be fully available for your child. It is also very important that dads and moms allocate time for each other and their children, collectively and separately. Alone time, or break time, needs to be allocated. Provided you are spending time with your children and making that quality time, they will not feel "so hungry" for you when you take time for yourself.

2. *When is it good to force your children to entertain themselves or participate in activities without you?*

The first instance would be when it is impossible for you to be present with them. For instance, when you are at work, too tired, or in a really bad mood. Your children need you to be there as much as possible.

Another good time to try to get children to entertain themselves is when there is fighting between siblings, or when they are withstanding an event which might be boring for them, such as a car ride. Encouraging your child to spend time doing things without you is a wonderful way to help keep them from missing you so much.

3. What are signs that you are spending too much or too little time with your children?

Signs that you are spending too much time with your child could be:

- your child is trying to get away from you or getting fresh with you;
- you are preferred to anyone else and they are not spending time with their friends;
- your other children are complaining that you are spending too much time with one of their siblings;
- your partner is also telling you that you are spending too much time with one child.

Signs that you are spending too little time with your child could be:

- they are telling you directly (hopefully);
- they are acting out;
- they are doing things in front of you to get your attention;
- they are getting into trouble at school;
- they are borrowing your things without asking.

CHAPTER 12

THE EFFECTS OF VIOLENT MEDIA ON REAL-LIFE VIOLENCE

EIGHT YEAR OLD BILLY, A GENERALLY WELL-MANNERED, bright boy, recently spent an hour watching an episode of a highly violent police show on television with his parents as an experiment to see if he could tolerate watching certain shows with them. His parents were hoping they could watch the same shows as a family without it having any negative effects on Billy. Soon after the episode ended, Billy had a hard time falling asleep that evening and then at 4:00 a.m. he awoke from a terrible nightmare. Although his parents were able to soothe him back to sleep, the next morning Billy was afraid to go to school. This was very unusual for him as he generally liked school and had never shown any resistance to going in the past. Through prodding and pushing, his parents were able to get Billy to school although he had a difficult time concentrating throughout the day. In the after-school program, a boy stole a ball from Billy, and he reacted by hitting the boy. Billy's parents were called, and Billy had to leave the program early that day. Billy is like many children who are otherwise calm and normally functioning in their development, but can be temporarily affected by information and pictures going beyond the capacity for a child to tolerate without becoming personally affected.

Until approximately a decade ago, many experts only inferred that the effects of violent media influenced real-life aggressive acts in children and adolescence. Due to a plethora of research conducted in this area, fact has replaced inference. Study after study has now confirmed that extensive viewing of violence, whether through the medium of television, video games, or the internet, causes greater aggressiveness in children and adolescents. Although some children are more sensitive and susceptible than others, occasionally even a single violent program can increase aggressiveness. Important findings have further concluded the following:

- The more realistic the violence (especially when frequently repeated or unpunished), the more likely it evokes children to mimic what they see.
- Children with emotional, behavioral, learning, or impulse control problems tend to be most influenced by the various mediums of violence.
- The effects of exposure may be immediate or delayed and are not necessarily related to conditions at home.
- Routine viewing of aggressive material by some children and adolescents may "immune" them or render them numb to the horror of violence.
- Many children who view violence gradually come to accept it as a means of solving problems.
- Viewing violence can make children less sensitive to the pain and suffering of others, more fearful of the world around them, and cause children to behave more aggressively towards others.

Children between the ages of 2 and 5 are still primarily conceptualizing their world in magical ways. When faced with aggressive scenes on television or on the computer, a child in this age range could well believe what they have viewed is real and might happen to them or their family. Consequently, this may evoke tremendous fear. The adolescent population is also particularly vulnerable to the external impact of aggression. Because of increasing levels of hormones, intensifying drives and desires to be powerful, exposure to overly aggressive and also overtly sexual material can lead to impulsiveness and poor judgment. While media violence is not the only cause of aggressive or violent behavior, it has been proven to be a significant contributing factor to unwanted aggression in children. Parents need to protect their children and adolescents from excessive exposure.

Key Points:

1. **Pay attention to what your child is watching or the games they are playing.**
2. **Set limits on both the amount and content of what your child is watching or playing.**
3. **Help children understand that there is a difference between television and real-life.**
4. **Refuse to allow children to watch or participate in activities that are not age-appropriate.**
5. **If offensive material comes on, change the channel, and discuss why such behavior is not a good idea.**
6. **Try to consult with the parents of your child's friends so there is consistency in the various households.**

FAQ's

1. How do I prepare my child for inevitable over-exposure in the media?

Be careful not to over-expose your child to media in their own house by screening what they see. It is important to look ahead to what will be broadcast on television, and screen it or turn it off while it is airing. This also applies to your computers. It is important to have protective firewalls enabled so that children cannot get into websites that you believe to be inappropriate for their age group. Firewalls by themselves are not enough; you should also place the computer in a room in the house where everyone can see the monitor. This will deter children from deviating from the approved sites because they know you could show up at any moment.

You do not have a lot of control over what goes on outside of your house unless you talk to other parents. However, remember that your children will learn the most from you, so if you present a good example of appropriate programming, it will be helpful for them no matter what they are exposed to outside the home.

2. What are the warning signs that my child's behavior is being influenced by negative media influences?

If there is a mimicking or a reenactment by the child of something they saw on television or a video game, it is a good sign their behavior was directly influenced. Another sign is if you see a change in your child's behavior after watching a program which may have been too violent or sexual. A good test to determine if this is the case is to remove the violent video game or movie, then pay close attention to any changes in their behavior. You can ascertain whether or not it was that medium or perhaps another agent that is causing their behavioral changes.

3. How do I avoid over-protecting my child to the point of naiveté?

Balance is everything. It is important your child be exposed to certain things on television so they can relate to their peers and have an idea of what is going on in the world. However, you don't want them to be so inundated as to cause a sense of over-stimulation and anxiety.

CHAPTER 13

PREPARING SIBLINGS FOR A NEW BABY

FOUR YEAR OLD CHRISTOPHER FELT LIKE THE KING OF his family. As the younger of two children, his sister Brittany was three years his senior, so he truly was the baby of the family. Everyone seemed to dote on him and this left him feeling very special and secure. In fact, he would brag to his friends and teachers that he was loved by everyone and his life was great. Shortly after turning four years old, he noticed his mother's tummy growing and decided to ask her about it. She was not sure when was the right time to let him know she was going to have another boy. Like most expectant parents, Christopher's mother was anticipating this would be a difficult acceptance for him so she was trying to push off the announcement for as long as possible. When she did tell him the wonderful news about having a little brother to play with, Christopher's initial reaction was that he had plenty of friends and did not need any more; he seemed hurt his mom had made a decision without asking him. For the next few months, Christopher's overall attitude changed; he became more moody, irritable, and even aggressive towards everyone. It is not uncommon that the announcement of a sibling created a regression for Christopher whereby he was in conflict over his feelings about a little brother and no longer being the baby in the family.

Bringing home a new baby is an adjustment for everyone, but the effect on the older brother or sister, depending upon their age and intellect, can be very confusing and very upsetting. The older children have experienced an individual bond with their parents involving less interference from their siblings which has made them feel special, loved, and as though they are an extension of their parents. It is not unusual for the older sibling to go through a time of regression once a baby has been brought home. They feel their standing with their parents has been replaced by another child. Their small egos have been hurt. Depending upon the age of the older sibling, each child will develop their own fantasy as to why they think their parents had another child. Many times the older brother or sister will think it was because they were not "good enough" or that their parents did not "love them" enough, leading to feelings of sadness and anger. This could manifest orally or behaviorally. Generally speaking, the older the sibling and the more developmentally mature he/she is when a new baby arrives, the easier it is for him or her to adapt to the new baby.

Despite most families having their children approximately two years apart, this range is probably the worst time to introduce a new baby. Children in the 12 to 24 month age group are in the process of trying to separate from their parents safely and are looking for support from them. They are in the active stage of trying to test their independence and look to their parents for loving assistance during this phase. When a new baby arrives, the sibling is not yet feeling comfortably independent and may react very strongly to the baby's introduction to the family. It is in this setting when they often make statements such as, "When is he or she leaving?" or "Make them go away." Once a child is through the 2 to 3 year old phase, he is better prepared for a new brother or sister. Three-to-five year olds are often identifying with their parents as "little men or women", may actually help in the process of parenting the newborn, and are more likely to be excited. They may still have feelings about no longer being the only child, but they are at a developmental level where they are better able to handle the change.

At any age, however, parents need to be very sensitive to the feelings of the older brother or sister when a new baby arrives. It is essential to make the older sibling feel "special" in their own right and make certain they are given plenty of love, attention, and admiration. Furthermore, the older child needs to see that because of their age, they receive certain privileges the younger ones do not receive, i.e. different toys, a bigger bed, etc. This helps them realize that being an older sibling is special.

It also helps to discuss the arrival of the baby prior to birth. Explaining to the older sibling that they will be getting a brother or a sister makes them feel as though they are part of the process. Assuring them you love them and that because they are so wonderful you wanted to have another child, also helps the older sibling understand the choice to have another child was not because you as parents were dissatisfied with them.

Most importantly, encourage the older child to talk to you about his or her feelings regarding the new baby and continue to spend ample one-on-one time as well as family time together. The more parents are aware of the sense of loss in their older child, the easier it will be for him/her to slowly adjust to a new member of the family.

Key Points:

1. Expect regression.
2. Prepare your child/children ahead of time.
3. Make your child feel special for being the oldest.
4. If you can, wait until the older child is over three years old before having another child.
5. Encourage your child to talk about the event.
6. Continue alone time with your child after the birth.

FAQ's

1. *How much regression should be tolerated?*

Regression is a normal part of this process. It is not a question of tolerating the regression; it is rather how to deal with it and how to help your child tolerate the advent of a new baby in the family. Obviously if your child is having a stronger reaction than most, then the introduction of a new baby has really caused them a lot of dismay and anxiety; they are telling you so through their regressive behavior. Regression needs to be met with a combination of understanding, empathy, and limit setting when necessary, to help the child cope with the changes and conflicts a new baby is going to bring the family.

2. *Is it more important to emphasize special alone time with the older sibling or should everything now revolve around family time?*

There needs to be a combination of both. There needs to be special alone time with the older sibling, special alone time with the baby, and family time as well, so it is not an either/or proposition, but an all-of-the-above situation.

3. What can the secondary caregiver do to ease this transition process?

Secondary caregivers can be really helpful in picking up the slack. They can be the one who spends extra time with the older sibling to take away the sadness and anger the child will have because the mother is not as available to him. On the other hand, the secondary caregiver can also be a reliever to the primary caregiver by taking care of the baby so they can spend time with the older sibling, which is also very important.

CHAPTER 14

PROFANITY AND CHILDREN

Although George Carlin was a brilliant man and fabulous comedian, his views on the "normalization" of profanity is one area of his reasoning with which I must respectfully disagree. For very good reason, the use of profanity has always been prohibited in schools, camps, sports clubs, and all organizations that work with youths. Most parents do not let their children swear because they intuitively know it is not in their child's best interests and can lead to all sorts of future problems.

When children are allowed to use curse words, they know within their minds it is wrong and that they are breaking a rule. Most healthy children feel bad when they break rules and unconsciously punish themselves in a variety of ways for not "doing what they are taught to do" by their parents, teachers, coaches, etc. The common term of "negative attention" can be applied to this concept. Aside from breaking a rule, the content of such words can also lead to greater impulsiveness, over-stimulation, and fighting within the household and on the playground. Swearing can also become infectious and other children, wishing to be accepted, will adopt such terminology.

Beneath the inappropriate use of curse words are obvious feelings and thoughts which parents must try to understand — without being judgmental or making their children feel guilty. Context is important. When a child uses a swear word to emphasize an emotion, parents need to discern the root of their child's feelings. A sexual context may be an indication their child has some questions or anxieties about such topics.

Therefore, it is important for parents to intervene in four ways when their children swear. Before setting a limit or punishing them, first try to listen to the context of their choice of words and ask yourself what they might be feeling and thinking. Second, validate the child's root feelings. Third, help your child get to the bottom of what is either bothering them or what might be on their mind. Finally, the helpful parent needs to set limits on the use of such words with constructive alternatives, encouraging the child to use more appropriate words to express their feelings. The basic idea behind this technique is not to instill guilt over their profanity, but to help them learn how to accept, manage, and express themselves in an appropriate manner. When successfully accomplished, the child feels supported, protected, and validated for his feelings which then reduces self-punishment, e.g. negative attention and other forms of behavioral or psychological problems.

The use of swear words provides the parent with an opportunity to educate their child about otherwise potentially inaccessible subject matter. For example, most children between the grades of 4 and 6 begin to use a variety of sexual terms and frequently take the terms too far. This is an indication that as "tweens" their bodies are changing and they are starting to experience new sensations which are confusing, exciting, and quite possibly, anxiety-provoking. When parents hear these types of terms, the door is opened to approach them with opportunities to discuss puberty and questions about topics such as masturbation etc. Once again, behind every expression of profanity are feelings, thoughts, and perhaps some anxiety about what is going on inside of their mind. Just punishing them for what they say misses the opportunity to help them learn about themselves, others, and how to better tolerate and express strong feelings. When parents approach profanity from a more understanding perspective, they are doing what all parents should be doing — parenting. Your children will surely benefit from it.

Key Points:

1. **Profanity is an expression of strong feelings and thoughts.**
2. **Parents need to try to understand what is behind the terms their child is using.**
3. **Profanity is an opportunity for parents to help children explore their questions.**
4. **Set limits on curse words, but encourage the expression of the feeling with other more appropriate words.**
5. **When children are allowed to "break rules" they feel bad about themselves and may go into a self-punishing mode behaviorally, academically, or otherwise.**

FAQ's

1. *What if my child is using language that is not yet age-appropriate for a more elaborate discussion?*

Try to find out where they are learning these words. If they are watching television shows which may include material that is too advanced, then it is definitely a matter you want to address. They may also be on a computer and getting into sites they should not have access to. The first question a parent has to ask is, "What are they trying to tell me by what they are saying?" Oftentimes when children are using sexual terms it's because they are starting to wonder about sex and because they are not feeling comfortable about it. They use age-inappropriate language because of their sense of discomfort. A savvy parent will both try to determine what their child might really be wondering and respond at a level the child can understand. Secondly, try to determine if there are external influences that may be over-stimulating for the child (television, computer, or a friend who is too old). If need be, at that point set limits.

2. *How do I handle family members or other guests who do not respect our home's language rules?*

Before guests or extended family members come to visit, it is always a good idea to discuss with them any family rules or moral values you practice so your guests have time to plan accordingly. However, if that does not work, it is important to avoid confusing your children. Therefore, you should consult with the member privately and discuss with them the significance of your family rules; hopefully they will support your efforts. If for some reason your guests do not support your values and theirs are too dissimilar, then it would be better for them to stay in a hotel close by your home. Planning ahead for conditions like this is always a good idea to avoid any conflicts which might arise during special family time such as the holidays.

3. *What is appropriate punishment for continued use of inappropriate language by an adolescent or "tween?"*

Obviously, if there is continued use of inappropriate language after a parent has set limits; there is more going on inside the child resulting in continued inappropriate speech and defiance of the rules. Perhaps they are angry or confused about something, or maybe even feeling badly about something they are thinking or doing. Unconsciously they are asking you to set limits to help them feel more in control. Considering this, it is always prudent to use the least restrictive means of punishment before proceeding into a continuum of greater ones. Give the child an opportunity not to lose more than necessary to help them to control themselves better.

Special Note: I tend not to look at things as punishment. I look at contingencies as the parental way of helping a child be a better boss of their feelings. In other words, we don't want to punish feelings because we don't want children to feel badly for expressing their feelings; we want to help them feel okay with feelings, but manage them more appropriately.

CHAPTER 15

CHANGE THE "TUDE"

It is a parent's worst nightmare. Evidence of an "attitude" is one that begins as early as two years of age and remains intact through ages 16 to 17. It frequently manifests when a child or adolescent is feeling thwarted, is in a bad mood, tired, or when interrupted or refrained from an activity of their choice. Many parents become angry and intolerant of their child's "tude" and insist it change or be altered, earlier rather than later. But they find that demanding such a change only serves to intensify the condition, creating even more tension around the house.

Although annoying and frustrating, the development of an attitude is in actuality a developmental achievement. Despite the annoyance, frustration, sense of disrespect and disruption in the household a belligerent adolescent or an obnoxious toddler can create, he or she is actually trying to demonstrate two opposing positions simultaneously: 1) a desire for independence, and 2) an attempt to prevent a fear of dependency on parents. Such internal conflicts (which are not conscious) can produce an attitude which is simply an attempt to protect the child from feeling vulnerable. In order to develop the "tude", the child has to actually progress developmentally and is not merely being difficult.

The observation of "tude" is most evident at three particular times in a child's development: between the ages of 2 to 4 (aka "the terrible twos"); ages 6 to 8; and once again from 12 to 15. These times illustrate when the child is shifting through what is termed the Separation-Individuation Phase of development. These are normal shifts representing psychological changes which are actually needed for the individual to eventually become a healthy adolescent and later adult. However, most parents do not understand the healthy function of attitude nor how best to deal with it when it becomes too intense or compromising to the child or adolescent.

STEPS FOR ADDRESSING THE "TUDE"

The first step for the parent is to understand the normality and function of attitude, namely that it is a good rather than a bad sign. This realization in itself will help the parent feel better and also lessen the intensity of their interactions. Next, the parent needs to try to better understand why the child or adolescent is presently in a "bad" mood or state and not take it personally. For example, most children and adolescents develop "the tude" when their parents introduce something they do not like, such as homework time, having to take a shower, having to abide by a curfew, or even going on a vacation together. The third step is telling, NOT asking, the child or adolescent how they think they are feeling based on their behavior or attitude. For example, when the parent tells the child they think their behavior is evidence they are feeling angry, and the parent is tolerant of the emotion, the child feels both informed and supported. This technique itself can temper the attitude. The child or adolescent is now aware that you know what is going on and are accepting of their feelings, and you can now ask them to express themselves in a more appropriate manner. In many cases, compliance will follow because they are both aware of how they are feeling, and in addition feel you understand. The final step is utilizing a limit or contingency, if necessary, designed to "help" the child manage their feelings, rather than feel bad about them.

When eight year old Timmy refused to take his evening shower, his mother initially responded by stating, "Timmy, I know you hate taking showers and are angry with me for making you take them, but it is important for your body to take one." Timmy calmed down after this sensitive statement, but continued to refrain from getting into the shower. His mother then stated "Timmy, your anger is okay, but you still need to take the shower. To HELP you manage your anger at me, if you don't get into the shower by the count of five, you will have to miss watching tonight's episode of *Sponge Bob*." Timmy thought about it for a moment and eventually got into the shower.

Although this example might seem simplistic, parents who use this technique report that their child's "tude" is much more tolerable than when they either avoid interacting with the child who's in a bad mood or merely threaten to punish their children when they act up. Whether a child is 2 or 14, they still need their parents to help them understand themselves and help them feel comfortable with their internal states of mind. Over time, this process becomes internalized and self-actualized, but usually not until late adolescence or early adulthood. In summary, when the "tude" is met with acceptance, understanding, communication, and guidance, its manifestation is greatly reduced, making households more functional through childhood and into adolescence.

Key Points:

1. Attitude is a healthy developmental achievement beginning at age two.
2. "Tude" is most evident between ages 2-4; 6-8; and 12-14.
3. To mellow the "tude", parents need to be understanding, knowledgeable, and guiding.
4. Don't take the "tude" personally and react with haste. Label the child's feelings and guide them into resolution.

FAQ's

1. When is an attitude the reflection of something more serious?

It may be a sign of something more serious when the attitude is matched with actions that are compromising some aspect of the child's or adolescent's life. For example, if the attitude is causing them to not have many friends, something is truly bothering the child; therefore making relationships or friendships is complicated to them. When an attitude overly compromises the child's or parent's life, it may be a reflection of something deeper and more complicated than just a poor choice of words.

2. How do I successfully discipline a teenager with attitude?

The first step is to align yourself with the concept that discipline is a form of love and helping, not hurting, and that it isn't the representation of anger, but concern for your child's best welfare. Such important realizations need to be communicated directly to the child so they *don't* feel like you don't understand them, and *do* understand you are not punishing their feelings. Taken together, the parent needs to explain to the teenager that their present attitude seems to be communicating difficulty they are experiencing in managing their life; that you, as the parent, are required by parental law (Ha!) to help them not do anything which could possibly complicate their full level of development and successfulness. A combination of empathy, understanding, and even perhaps agreeing with whatever is bothering them is required, followed with helpful limits to drive home the point. The successful parent is always invested in their child's optimum level of growing and being happy.

3. *What happens when punishments don't work?*

Either you are not getting to the root of the problem, or your child is seeking punishment because he is not feeling good about himself, or your punishments are not meaningful enough to the child. For some children a warning is enough; for others taking away almost everything except their bed frame has to happen before the child feels the parent really loves and cares for him.

CHAPTER 16

AVOIDING BABYSITTER NIGHTMARES

In San Diego, an eleven year old sister was convicted of killing her younger sibling while babysitting alone at home. Although tragedies such as this one are very rare, many parents have had negative experiences with babysitters or when allowing older siblings to care for their younger brothers or sisters. I field many questions on this subject: "At what age is it safe for an older sibling to baby-sit for younger siblings?" "What characteristics should we look for when hiring a babysitter?" "Should we have a number of different sitters or just a select one or two?" These three sample questions highlight the importance of being very careful and thoughtful when leaving your children in someone else's trust.

The following is a list of qualifications all babysitters must have at any age in order to fulfill the necessary requirements of caring for a child when parents are not supervising:

- At least average intelligence;
- Very good judgment;

- Intact morals;
- Emotional stability;
- A capacity to manage stressful situations;
- Knowledge of what to do in an emergency;
- Patience.

As one can see from this list these characteristics demonstrate a certain level of maturity which many children (and some adults) have not mastered. In any case, these characteristics are not expected until at least middle to late adolescence (14 to 17 years of age). Therefore, allowing a child under this age group to baby-sit alone is not recommended and can lead to problems.

Allowing siblings to baby-sit each other is another important consideration each parent must evaluate before permitting it. In some situations the result is fine, but in others this is not the case. All siblings have conflicts with one another as they must manage feelings of competition, envy, and frustration, balanced with love and caring for their brother or sister. How each child manages these "normal conflicts" will result in how they treat their siblings. In some cases, despite these everyday internal conflicts, the behavior of the sibling is well-managed and controlled, but in other cases the behavior manifests in aggression and acting out. Older siblings who can manage these conflicts well might be good candidates to baby-sit, while those who cannot are better not left in a situation alone with their brother or sister.

Finally, in reference to the question of having numerous babysitters versus a select few, this is a personal choice. As long as the necessary requirements are fulfilled to ensure safety and responsibility, the number of babysitters can vary. My bias, however, is that a select few is preferable due to the attachments children make to adults. Children become accustomed to adults in their lives and a consistent adult can be very helpful to their continued development, much like that of a teacher. Furthermore, seeing a consistent face or two will earn more respect than meeting too many and this can lead to greater respect and compliance — think substitute teacher. However, if you have more than three children in the home, it would be a good idea to use two sitters together rather than one, in order to reduce competition and keep things calmer.

Many cities have programs which actually train adolescents to become "certified" babysitters. Obviously a child who dedicates his or her time to learn more about how to take care of children would probably fulfill the needed requirements to care for younger children and would be a good choice. However, before hiring any babysitter, go through the checklist previously mentioned and get answers to these questions so the safety of your child is ensured.

Key Points:

1. **All babysitter candidates should meet your standards.**
2. **Choosing a good match for your children should be subjective.**
3. **Despite their age, older siblings are not always a good choice.**
4. **Consistency with babysitters is preferable.**

FAQ's

1. Should I use a hidden baby cam for my sitters?

Some people swear by baby cams and feel they are the best way to make sure whoever is caring for their child is doing a good job.

However, you have to consider how your nanny would feel not only about being filmed, but about not being trusted. If they find the camera, it could be a problem on many levels. A lot depends on your babysitter. He/she should be someone you know, have met and interviewed, and someone whose references you have checked. He/she should be someone you have heard feedback from other adults and children they have provided service for, as well as being someone who seems to like and be liked by your children. If everything checks out and they are over the age of 16, there might not be a reason to have a hidden baby cam. However, if you have unfortunately had some bad experiences and you are worried it may happen again, a baby cam could be helpful as an initial screening process for a sitter.

2. *Should I prepare activities or leave it up to my sitter to entertain my children?*

This really depends on the individual care giver. Some sitters come with a bag of tricks; you don't have to do anything and they relate well to your children which is great when this happens. You have likely already interviewed the sitter in your home; they have had a chance to see your playroom, and are able to come up with some great ideas and games. However, it is always a good idea to have activities or games for all ages already in your home and inform the sitter of what is available. You also want to let the sitter know you want him/her to supervise all of the play time so no one gets hurt or in trouble.

3. *Should I allow my sitter to discipline my kids or do it myself, as necessary, when I return?*

It is really important that parents empower the babysitter as the disciplinarian when they are not there. This is another reason why you want to make sure your sitter is of a certain maturity so he/she is capable and up to the task of setting limits; that he/she will discipline and will not co-mingle with your child. You are leaving the babysitter in a position of authority. It is also important the sitter and the children know that if something does happen you will get the full story from the sitter so you can follow up once you get home.

CHAPTER 17

ASSIGNING CHORES

ONE BASIC PARENTAL CONSIDERATION INVOLVES THE implementation of chores. Although most parents assign chores to their children at some point during their development, there is variability as to what age this should begin and what particular chores are appropriate for children at various ages. The assignment of chores for children helps to develop three basic fundamentals: self-responsibility, independence, and teamwork.

Although invaluable, it is important to consider two factors before introducing chores to children. These factors include: 1) the child's developmental capacity, and 2) how the type of chore chosen will affect the child's feelings and attitude. Regarding developmental capacity, it is important not to ask a child to perform any task that they are not yet developmentally capable of performing. Doing so will create a sense of inferiority, guilt, and shame. Fundamentally, most children are not capable of performing any routine chore until the later stage of early childhood (5 to 6 years or age). If a parent desires a child of this age to have chores, they must be very simple and easy to perform. Furthermore, the parent will often have to frequently remind their young child to do the task and will often need to help them complete it. Typically, tasks such as cleaning up after themselves and making their bed are two of the most common beginning chores assigned by parents. As children become older and more developmentally functional, parents can introduce new tasks for completion, but initially, they will need to help their child become accustomed to the chore and help them adjust to the change.

Regarding the type of chore chosen by the parent, it is important not to pick chores involving the following: 1) preparing complicated meals for themselves; 2) chores involving activities that could lead to a very negative outcome; and 3) performing chores which are very upsetting. For instance, cleaning up after animals on a routine basis should not be assigned until the child is an adolescent who can make the connection to responsibility rather than associate the chore with how the parent feels about the child by asking him to perform an unpleasant act. Chores are designed to help children learn to become more independent and self-responsible, not to replace the function of good parenting which involves primary caretaking, protecting children, and being sensitive to their strong feelings.

"Should parents reward children for doing chores?" The answer to this question is "Yes." Most children will initially resist doing chores for a number of different reasons, but once they witness their accomplishment they tend to feel good about themselves. Parents who commend their children with encouraging words such as, "I'll bet it felt great to you to see you could do that", helps their child develop an inner world of self-praise. Establishing an allowance is also fine and gives children something to look forward to. It allows them the opportunity to use some of their own money to buy little items which reinforce their personal accomplishments.

Over time, the type of chores can gradually advance and should meet the developmental progression of the child. If done in this fashion, the parent is helping their child become more self-functional and promoting a sense of self-efficacy. In the end, the child learns both how to better self-manage and also the importance of working together with their family as a unit which ideally gets passed along to the next generation.

Key Points:

1. **Chores are an important part of your child's healthy development.**
2. **Make sure your child is able to physically and mentally accomplish any chores you assign.**
3. **Be willing to work with your child to complete a chore and to make it a comfortable part of their routine.**
4. **Your child's chores should never replace any of your fundamental duties as caregiver.**

FAQ's

1. *What if my child refuses to do chores or does not do them satisfactorily?*

Most children are not going to do chores unless you pay them to do them. At most ages, chores are another thing a child has to do when already feeling bogged down with school work. When you assign chores, a child feels you do not understand just how complicated and busy their life is. Chores for children are not a bad idea, but it is also important they can earn something for doing them and they can earn a little bit more if their chores are done really well. When compensated with money or some other reward or treat, children often perform much better and it leads to them feeling better about themselves. In some cases, however, if you are asking your child to do a chore which is too complicated for him like feeding your dogs correctly, because of his developmental level the result will be his feeling poorly about himself and his abilities.

2. Should chores be used as a punishment tool?

They can be. It depends on what the chore is. As long as it is not some sort of heinous chore for a small child such as having to pick up dog poop. A parent can certainly utilize chores as a way of helping the child remember to be a better boss of his feelings. Chores are a better choice of punishment than some parents realize.

3. If we have a housekeeper and my children's schedules are filled with activities, is there a substitute for chores?

There is only so much a child can do. If they are extremely busy with school and extracurricular activities, there may not be time for chores. The point of chores is to developmentally increase the complexity over time. You want to give chores to children as they are functionally starting to take care of themselves and can actually do them. For example, when your five year old is now using the toilet to go to the bathroom, there is nothing wrong with assigning the chore of making sure he puts the toilet seat down after he is finished. You have to make sure the chores you give are learning moments; if the child is busy, give them a couple of chores; if they are not busy you can give them a little bit more to do. Just make it worth their while to complete them.

CHAPTER 18

FIELDING QUESTIONS FROM YOUR CHILDREN

Every parent has the same experience — being bombarded with a plethora of questions from their child arising shortly after they learn to talk, increasing during the childhood years, and then tapering down during adolescence. With each of these interactions comes the concern for what is the "right" or "wrong" thing to say based on a balance between the message the parent wishes to convey and the parent's concern for how their child will digest the information.

To complicate this further, the very same question a four year old asks his parents has a very different meaning when it is asked by a 10 year old. Likewise, the response from the parent needs to take into consideration these developmental differences. Although a child has an inborn drive to learn about his world, his young mind is only able to digest and utilize information he is able to comprehend at his particular age. We call this "functional development." For example, if a child is given too much information at too young an age, the well-intended information may actually cause more harm than good. On the other hand, too little information, or a complete avoidance of the topic, may leave the child feeling insecure about what they asked or lead them to continue to seek the information from a far less suitable source.

The key point here is that when children ask questions, they need answers as they attempt to understand their minds and the world around them. The role of the parent is to supply enough adequate information without overwhelming them with details beyond their developmental level, or not giving them enough information to satisfy their curiosity.

But how do parents know what is too much or just enough, based on the developmental level of their child? Most parents do not have degrees in child development and there is no guidebook about right versus wrong answers. Part of the answer is common sense; the other part is trying to learn more about what children at different ages are able to comprehend. Many times parents also learn from trial and error. For instance, they may answer a particular question which results in making the child more anxious. Typically this type of experience helps the parent learn that their well-intended answer may have been too much for their child to process; the next time they are more careful. On the other hand, if the answer is not sufficient for the child, he will continue to repeat the question until the parent meets his need.

Most parents want to be honest and give adequate information — this is a good rule of thumb. What is considered adequate, however, has to be adjusted to the age and developmental level of the child. Answers need to be clear and informative, but not beyond what the child can understand at his age. For example, when a five year old asks his mom or dad "Where do babies come from?" (which is a frequent and important question as they are asking about themselves), giving information about sex and body parts would be potentially overwhelming and could cause anxiety and even impulsivity. This type of reasoning is beyond what they are able to comprehend. When children are exposed to information too advanced for them, symptoms can develop and we see the same types of manifestations when children are exposed to television too graphic for them to grasp. Instead, teach young children that when mothers and fathers love each other, they have children to celebrate their love. This is often enough for the inquisitive five year old to feel satisfied with their question.

Obviously, the same question posed by a pre-adolescent would warrant a different response based on the pre-teen's added knowledge and ability to comprehend. In this instance, parents can begin to talk to their children about their bodies, lay some ground work about sexuality, and share the ideas of love, caring, and maturity. For discussions about sexuality and bodies with pre-teens (10 and older) and adolescents, I always suggest the parent of the same sex be the one to chair the meeting to lessen potential anxiety for the child. There are also a variety of books written for the pre-teens and teenagers about sexuality which can be very helpful for the inquisitive child. However, once again, parents need to be careful to not give too much or too little information at this age as well. Reading over a book before handing it over to your child is another good idea. Sensible, matter of fact, and "just enough" information to satisfy the question is the best method. Children are wonderful at telling us if they are not satisfied; they will just keep asking if we do not give them what they "need."

Key Points:

1. **Do not avoid answering your child's questions.**
2. **Answer questions with consideration for their age and developmental level.**
3. **Do not give children "too much" information, but just enough to satisfy them.**

4. **Refer to third party materials to help you teach them if necessary.**
5. **The same question will arise again at later dates allowing for more information to be given at that time.**

FAQ's

1. *How do I "unring a bell" to an age-inappropriate question to which my child already has misinformation?*

That is exactly what you tell your child: "Whatever you heard wasn't right and I am happy to clarify what I think you are talking about." However, your clarification and accurate information should not be so much that it over-stimulates the child and is only based on their particular question.

2. *What if my child knows way more than what I want to talk about?*

In all likelihood he will tell you, "Been there, know that." He is telling you he is able to hear a little bit more than perhaps you thought he was capable of learning. This leaves you in the position of educating him just a little bit more than you thought you would have to. But again, be careful to only take it to the level he seems to know about and leave it there.

CHAPTER 19

AVOIDING PATERNAL POSTPARTUM DEPRESSION FOR FIRST-TIME FATHERS

ED WAS ELATED WHEN HIS WIFE OF THREE YEARS ANNOUNCED she was finally pregnant. The couple had been trying to get pregnant for two years and was becoming very concerned that they would not be able to parent children. Fertility consultants had recommended medication to help them along, but because of some negative family experiences with past medications, they decided to continue to try to conceive naturally. However, the attempts had become anxiety provoking and "not much fun" as both Ed and his wife, Ellen, would base their intimacy on an ovulation schedule rather than spontaneity. Nevertheless, they had both concluded it was worth it if they could have a child together.

For Ed, the idea of becoming a father was wonderful. Although he had lost his own father in a traffic accident when he was 10 years old and his mother did not remarry, he thought having children would "complete his life" and give him the chance to provide a degree of fatherhood which his own father was unable to provide. Ed was also an only child and was hopeful he and Ellen would be able to have at least two children so his children could enjoy a life with siblings. He and his mother had a very close bond and Ed felt as though he was always at the center of her world. He also envisioned that having a baby would additionally deepen his love and intimacy with Ellen.

Ellen, the youngest of three children, was raised in an intact family. She had solid relationships with both of her parents and siblings, and wanted to raise a family in a similar fashion to the one in which she grew up. She was accustomed to sharing her parent's attention with her siblings and was excited about the idea of extending her immediate family with Ed.

Throughout the pregnancy, Ellen and Ed continued to bond and were sexually intimate with one another well into her second trimester. However, during Ellen's third trimester she developed back pain and no longer felt physically up to making love. This created conflict for Ed. On the one hand, he had compassion for Ellen's plight, but he also felt somewhat frustrated that they were temporarily unable to stay connected sexually.

The birth of the baby was a celebration for both Ed and Ellen. Together they joined in the expression of their love for one another and began to discuss immediate plans for taking care of baby Diane and future plans for their family. Ellen chose to breastfeed on demand and Diane began to immediately bond with Ellen; the two of them fell in love. Ed too, felt close to Diane, but began to feel a bit left out. He found himself feeling conflicted between elation about being a father and frustration about the dynamics having changed. No longer was he the center of Ellen's attention; he had to share her with his infant daughter. As Ed was an only child, sharing the key female figure in his life was something he had never had to experience.

To further complicate matters, like most infants, Diane was awake almost every two hours to nurse. Ed's sleep became disrupted as they kept Diane in a crib in their bedroom to make it easier for

Ellen. Ed was tired most mornings for the first four months until Diane was able to sleep through the night. Sex was on hold for the initial eight weeks, which was also difficult for Ed. It was a primary way for him to feel closer to Ellen and he began to take her inability to be sexual too personally. As a first time father, Ed was not anticipating that as Diane matured, his relationship with Ellen would once again become intimate and their relationship would broaden as they parented together. Instead, Ed was feeling confused. He loved his new baby, but was a bit sad, resentful, and worried about his future with Ellen in reference to their intimacy. Ellen, on the other hand, was "the happiest she had ever been." Her life felt complete. She had a loving husband and a baby who was in love with her — life was at its best.

The description above is a common example of what happens in many, if not most, first time families, when each parent anticipates what to expect during and after pregnancy. In fact, the literature on "what to expect when they are expecting" is more plentiful for upcoming mothers than for fathers in terms of the changes and challenges in both their relationship with their spouse and the changing family unit.

For the father, the birth of a child is both wonderful and naturally compromising. The gift of a child supplies a movement into a new developmental phase, fatherhood, which is filled with gratifications and responsibilities. But it also causes change in the basic family dynamic. In other words, the couple becomes a family, causing an extension of each individual's love, attention, and caring beyond the couple onto a child. The father will commonly feel a bit left out of the picture, even a bit rejected, as the new baby is bonding with the mother. This feeling typically lasts until about one year of age when the baby begins to seek out others to associate with, namely the father.

A parent's childhood experiences also play a part in how the father will manage these changes. In Ed's case, being an only child without a father provided him with the undivided attention of his mother throughout his childhood and adolescent development. This dynamic was then repeated in his relationship with Ellen until she became pregnant with Diane. For the first time in his life, Ed now had to share a mother figure, which was an unfamiliar experience for him. Feelings of envy and competition, mixed with love and admiration towards both Ellen and Diane, would be expected. For Ed, receiving some insight into both his personal experiences and the process of fatherhood during infancy would have surely helped him get through this period and improved his ability to cope and relate. For other fathers, particularly those who have had siblings growing up, the advent of a new baby reintroduces unconscious sibling rivalry. Depending upon how well this was tolerated and managed during childhood and adolescence will predict how the father will relate to a new baby who is competing with him for the attention of his wife/mother.

In extreme cases, some fathers will become depressed during the first year after the birth of their new babies — a male form of Postpartum Depression. This is usually due to unconscious feelings of anger and resentment regarding the losses and changes evident in their lives since having a new baby. However, most fathers who educate themselves about fatherhood, through either reading or talking with their peers, often offset any depressive condition. They tend to manage their conflicting feelings of love and loss well enough to participate fully in being a new father and expanding their relationship with their spouse.

Over time, fathers tend to habituate and adapt to the "new" family lifestyle. During the second year of their baby's life, the role of the father becomes very important. Most toddlers will reach out to their fathers as a way of separating from their mother. Most fathers love when this happens. Their relationship with their spouse further broadens to include children, and intimacy returns, although perhaps not as frequently due to the responsibilities of raising small children and the level of investment and fatigue most parents experience. However, as the children grow and mature, the couple may return to the early days of intimacy and increased time together.

Key Points:

1. **Fatherhood introduces gains and losses.**
2. **Most new fathers feel happy, sad, and rejected.**
3. **Family of origin issues predict how a new father will adapt to a new baby.**
4. **Postpartum Depression can occur among fathers as well as mothers.**
5. **Fathers who educate themselves about what to expect tend to thrive.**

FAQ's

1. *What steps can I take to help my husband better connect with our child during pregnancy?*

If your husband is like most men, he is conflicted between being elated to be a husband and becoming a father, but sad and dismayed about the time his wife will be spending with the baby. It is a humbling experience for most fathers. When the parents are able to spend some one-on-one time together, husbands tend to bond much better with their children.

If this is not the issue and you have a husband who may just be uncomfortable around children, then you may have to encourage him to have time alone with the baby. Stress how important fathers are to babies and how you need his help so you can go out to a movie with a friend. It is important you let fathers know their position is invaluable both to the baby and to you; ask him to help you. If he says he doesn't know what to do, then can give him some suggestions. With infants it may be nothing more than rocking and holding them, or perhaps going for a jog with the baby in a stroller (as long as it is safe). Mothers have to realize the regression which may occur with their husbands and accept that they will have two, and not one, children for a little while.

2. *How do I prepare my husband for the responsibilities and expectations of fatherhood?*

Hopefully, you have talked about this before you decided to have children. Pick up some books on child development and what to expect for the next 18 years. Really talk about what it was like growing up for both of you and reliving some of those experiences together so you have an idea of what you can expect. You also want to make sure you spend time with other families who have children so you can observe their behavior and talk to them. The more information you have ahead of time and the more you talk about it, the better prepared everyone will be.

3. *How do I jumpstart my husband out of his PPD funk?*

Intimacy helps, as does regular date nights with each other. Your husband needs to realize it is a not a choice you make between him *and* the baby; that he is still important and you still need him. Albeit the relationship changes quite a bit because now there are three and not two, you are united as parents for the well-being of your baby. Because of the joint requirements of caring for your baby, you are not going to be as intertwined as you used to be, or have the energy you used to have. But if you take some private time together, maybe have someone sit with your child so you can spend some time together, things tend to change for the better.

CHAPTER 20

DRESS-UP AND ROLE-PLAYING DEVELOPMENT

MOST PARENTS FIND IT AMUSING WHEN THEIR 3 TO 5 year olds transition into magical and creative play, which often includes dressing up in a variety of costumes. Such attire manifests itself in everything from superheroes and princesses to a variety of adult figures, including little mothers and fathers engaging in themes ranging from rescue, romanticism, and compassion, to destruction, conflicts, and even mock arguments. What most parents do not understand is that such play is a window into a child's mind and indicates where they are developmentally.

Before the age of three a child is typically still working out the kinks of toddler-hood which is the stage of development preceding what is referred to as early childhood. Toddlers are struggling to find a balance between the expected needs of dependence on mom and dad versus an inclination to be bigger and more independent. The play of the toddler is more about control, power, and fear; it infrequently has to do with themes of relationships and gender, which is what changes radically for most 3 to 5 year olds as they enter early childhood.

As with any age, play is symbolic of psychological growth and is the child's way of practicing new methods of understanding their minds, relationships, and the world around them. The dress-up play of the 3 to 5 year old in particular represents three new developmental themes: gender role identification; the growing and changing of interpersonal relationships; and conscience development. Such changes are made possible when the toddler years have been successful and the child has become more comfortable with him or herself and does not feel so "little" anymore. The "big boy" or "big girl" bed is often a metaphor for bigger and more expansive ways of understanding themselves and others. Dress-up play then becomes their mechanism for practicing these newfound attributes.

By about age three, from the gender identification point of view, boys and girls become more comfortable and aware of their bodies, recognizing the differences between the sexes and the differences in their own bodies from the other sex. This pushes boys and girls to look to others of the same sex for information and affirmation of their gender role. For example, many 3 to 4 year old boys become increasingly interested in their father's activities and frequently wish to engage with him. The translation in dress-up is often displayed by little boys dressing up as fathers, workmen, superheroes, and firemen, and their behavior is practiced to help them enjoy their new wishes and identification. For girls, the princess, mother, school teacher, dancer, and business person represent the same role playing for their gender. Of course, much has to do with the gender orientations and beliefs of the parents, for the child will internalize and mimic most often what his or her parent or parents emulate. Therefore, gender identification is complex. The parents "beliefs" in what boys and girls "should" play with is very important and becomes communicated to, and ingrained in the child.

Dress-up play also helps children practice their new development in relationships with others. Perhaps the most drastic change from toddler-hood to early childhood for most children is how they attempt to relate to more than one other person simultaneously. Before this time, relating to others was mainly one-on-one. In real life, this is represented by the child having a different relationship and interaction with each parent. In dress-up play, "playing house" often encapsulates this theme whereby the children have multiple roles such as husband, wife, mother and father. The acts and roles the children display are a way for them to become more comfortable with growth and change.

Finally, dress-up play also serves to help children learn rules and morals which shape their conscience. Most dress-up play themes, despite being magical in content, have rules by which the players abide, demonstrating that the child's conscious is in a period of formal development. Over time, such rule regiments become more intricate and serve to change the magical themes of the play to more realistic ones. Subsequently, dress-up play tends to fade away once the child's imaginative mind shifts into middle childhood where the child's thinking is more reality and rule-based. This transition into early childhood is reinforced through their earlier investment in trying on different outfits and personas.

Key Points:

1. **Dress-up play is a normal and healthy tool of development.**
2. **Dress-up play helps to consolidate three developmental functions:**
    a. **gender identification and integration;**
    b. **interpersonal or social development;**
    c. **conscience development.**

3. Parental attitude will have a strong effect on how the child understands and internalizes these functions.

FAQ's

1. At what age should dress-up and role playing end?

Typically dress-up and role playing are part of the stage we call magical thinking. It predominantly resides in a fantasy world. Children generally transition into more reality-based thinking from 5½ to 6 years of age. It is usually around this time that we see fantasy dress-up and role playing decrease, and more reality based activities such as sports, being with friends, and participation in activities that are daily based begins. This can be a sobering experience for many children as they realize the things that they thought were real turn out not to be, such as Santa Claus, the Easter Bunny, and the Tooth Fairy. But they also get excited about participating in age-appropriate activities where they can develop greater skills and talents.

2. Should I be worried about any signs in role playing which would suggest gender identification issues?

It is very common for small children between toddler-hood and middle childhood to play with dolls of both genders. In fact, out of curiosity and identification, some small children may play more with the opposite gender based toy. Over time the play usually takes on a more balanced atmosphere wherein there is an interchange of dolls of both genders. Typically the gender identification becomes more solidified by age five. There could be concerns if your child does seem to identify with a doll of the opposite gender and if this perpetuates past middle childhood (5 to 7 years old).

3. Should parents participate in/encourage role play and dress-up?

Play is a wonderful way of educating children about the world. In fact, I encourage parents to play with their children at all ages. During role play and dress-up, parents can act out certain characters as a way of teaching their child anything from morals to social skills. However, it is also really important to allow children to have free play without you so they can play out all sorts of ideas and fantasies without interruptions.

CHAPTER 21

DEVELOPING STUDY SKILLS

TWELVE YEAR OLD PATRICIA HAS HISTORICALLY BEEN a good student who relished the fact that she never had to study very much to get good grades. Her consistent success in school and with test performances gave her the feeling studying was for others and not her because of her ease in grasping academic material. However, soon after beginning middle school Patricia found herself struggling academically; what was being expected of her was beyond her immediate memory capacity. For the first time in her life she had to actually study both the material she heard in the classroom and what she read for homework. Because of Patricia's false sense of academic invulnerability, she was ill-prepared to begin middle school in terms of study habits and being able to organize her material. Up until this point her parents didn't need to help her learn how to study, take notes, and prepare for exams. As with most elementary school programs, there were no classes or instructions in developing study skills, so by the time Patricia entered middle school she was not ready for the changes in academic requirements and performance measures she had not had to deal with in her earlier years.

One of the strongest predictors of successful school performance is the child's capacity to study and complete assignments. In fact, children who have the finest study skills tend to obtain the best grades and get into the better colleges and universities, commonly resulting in occupational and personal success. Study skills involve tasks such as in-class note taking, organization, planning ahead, material integration, focused attention, and the completion of assignments. It is well-known that most schools place significant emphasis on these activities and base a large percentage of the class grades on the child's mastery of these abilities.

The development of study skills is not automatically acquired by most children. These are skills which must be initially taught then monitored before they become internalized and practiced independently by the child. Many parents rely on their child's school to teach these skills when deemed necessary and appropriate. Usually after a deficient report card the parents become involved, angry that the school did not teach their child how to study. They then battle with their child over the completion of assignments and the correlation between studying and getting good grades.

The age of the child and the length of time they have failed to develop adequate study skills will often determine how the child reacts when the parents become involved. Typically, the longer the child has failed to develop adequate study habits, the more resistant he will be to changing his behavior. This is most commonly observed in both middle school and high school. In such cases, many parents end up seeking academic assistance, such as a tutor, to help their child learn how to study. They also set limits involving desired activities until homework and studying are completed. Over time, if the parents remain consistent and serious, most children and adolescents do learn how to study and become organized.

Parents who begin in the early years of child rearing by teaching the importance of studying and homework, along with direct instruction on how to perform these tasks to their children tend to avoid these problems. Their child will have internalized and practiced good study habits early in their academic lives. Typically the child's school introduces homework in either first or second grade. This is the time when the parent needs to begin assisting their child with learning to organize, plan, and complete their assignments in settings which are free from distraction and optimal for studying. Because the child is just beginning to understand school, and is still eager to please the parent, most small children will be less resistant to working together with their parents on study skills. They will then feel proud when they witness their success as they receive a good grade from their teacher and accolades from their parents. Furthermore, because these skills were introduced early, "good" rather than "bad" study habits have been developed and become everyday routine. It is thereafter a matter of maintaining rather than breaking a habit.

Key Points:

1. **Teach study skills at an early age in the home.**
2. **Establish a homework time by second grade.**
3. **Develop an optimal homework environment and study area.**
4. **Schedule a break after school before homework.**
5. **Check over the homework assignments and projects.**
6. **Reward the completion of homework.**
7. **If bad habits manifest, take immediate action to prevent failure.**

FAQ's

1. *How do I get past having to hover over my child to get him to do his homework?*

To begin with, you introduce the idea of a good work ethic having to do with school very early on in their development. I usually suggest that once children start to have homework you set them up with a quiet study space, usually in their room with good lighting. Initially assist them by working through the homework if necessary, as well as by teaching them how to get organized, structured and scheduled in getting work done.

You have to work with your children to do this; they do not develop these skills on their own. If done early enough you will decrease your battle with your children in the years to come. Bad habits can develop early; parents often decide to get involved in homework too late when their child already has a very hard habit to break. This frequently results in "hovering" to make sure they actually get the work done. The ability of children to self-manage their work is another example of how, when children feel good about things they do well, their self-esteem and their work ethic tend to be very positive.

2. *Should I concern myself with my child's study habits as long as their grades are good?*

Many children, by virtue of good genes, are able to get their work done without having to study. However, usually by middle school and high school years even those children who have smart genes can start to do poorly if they do not know how to study and develop good habits. It is essential that study habits are taught very early in life, as early as the child can understand them. They will become more developed over time through the help of their parents and hopefully the school, so that those smart children who didn't used to have to study will learn solid habits for life and continue to do well.

3. I consider school to be my child's job. Why should I reward them?

Plain and simple: you want to reward your children for taking good care of themselves. That's their biggest chore. When children feel good about themselves and you reward them, you are communicating to them that they are important and that they are doing a good job. You are helping them see the worth in themselves and the value of taking care of themselves. This will only result in enhanced feelings of self-worth and success both in grade school and eventually in college.

CHAPTER 22

HELPING CHILDREN GET BACK INTO SCHOOL – HOLIDAY DAZE & SUMMER SLUMP

THE HOLIDAY DAZE

READJUSTING TO SCHOOL AFTER THE HOLIDAYS OR summer vacation is anything but an easy task. Children don't think about starting school until the day before school starts unless the parents bring it up. Because of their disdain for having to switch from doing things that are fun and enjoyable to getting back into a routine and going back to work, they tend not to think about the change ahead in order to prepare themselves accordingly. Therefore, their reaction to going back to school is harder than those who are informed ahead of time that a change is on the horizon.

If your family is like most, your children are in a state of denial when they are about to go back to school. As parents, however, you are ready for the holidays to end and excited about getting them back into structure and routine. Many parents avoid the concept of talking to their children about school restarting for fear of putting them into bad moods and getting into a fight with them. On the other hand, when parents do not approach talking about getting ready for school again and looking ahead to expectations for success, the avoided conflicts tend to emerge anyway. Shortly after school resumes, problems arise or repeat themselves from the previous term. In addition, when parents do not discuss this upcoming change, children often go into a short-term slump due to the lack of mental preparation and a mini-bout of post-vacation depression.

As with any transition, preparing ahead of time is always a good idea. When situations are thought through, discussed, and planned for, there tends to be less anxiety generated and a greater likelihood for success. Young children in particular are not yet capable of thinking in the abstract to plan ahead. They need assistance in understanding what is expected of them and how to reach their goals. Many times parents place responsibilities on their children which they are not able to developmentally manage and which can set their child up for failure. The responsibilities of school are common areas where parents either expect their child to manage themselves, or rely on the school to teach them how to organize and study.

Each January, after the holidays, represents opportunities for parents to discuss change and goals for the new year. Parents of both grade and middle school students need to sit down with their children and discuss expectations and plans for how to help them succeed. Reviewing the importance of school, your faith in their abilities to manage their work, and discussing concepts such as studying, organization, and note-taking, are all essential to making sure your child feels prepared. Oftentimes after such discussions the parents and child determine areas needing some assistance for which their talk served to provide a platform for action. Self-esteem is generated when a child experiences success. When children have the tools necessary to manage their life, success is more likely. On the other hand, if your child is doing well, be sure to pat him or her on the back and express how happy you are for them.

Structure is also very important. Children and adolescents who have a daily "routine" tend to do better academically and socially. For example, it is always a good idea to have an after-school plan which entails: 1) an after-school snack; 2) some time for play or sport; and 3) a scheduled homework time to be performed in a distraction-free environment. Once homework has been completed, a "reward" time can be offered to celebrate getting through their assignments after a long day of school. When children have something to look forward to, they tend to feel less frustrated and seem more motivated.

For the high school student who can think in the abstract and hopefully understand that their success at this time of their academic life will serve later goals, discussions should be presented in which you are allowing them to tell you how they plan to manage their school work. This will make them feel as though you respect their intellect and acknowledge their prior success. If, however, you determine they do not seem able to manage themselves well enough, you will have to help them. Setting up children and adolescents to "learn from their mistakes" is poor judgment on the part of the parent, because the child and adolescent is not yet mature enough to manage their lives independently without parents.

THE SUMMER SLUMP

By mid-summer, parents are typically becoming frustrated with their children sitting around the house, sleeping until noon, watching endless hours of television, or being online with their friends. Within a month of school starting again, parents get nervous about how well their children will re-adapt to academia given their recent summer vacation. I recommend "balancing summers" with fun activities, some academic or literary exposure, as well as family time. I recognize that due to several circumstances this cannot always take place. However, there is still time to help your child balance their day in preparation for beginning school in the fall. In fact, research shows that parents who are sensitive to their child's need to relax, but who also demand some structure, produce children who are higher achievers.

Most children and adolescents are not independently capable of arranging responsible summer plans. Parents need to mandate certain activities and follow through with implementation. This is heightened if the child is in the grips of the "Summer Slump." In this case, sitting down with your child and coming up with a plan for the rest of the summer is essential, keeping in mind that you are trying to help them get re-acquainted with the expectations of school in September. Parents will thank themselves later because they are helping their children integrate balance, which is essential for successful school performance. Getting them into some sort of camp, mandating recreational reading, helping set up play dates, and taking a family vacation are all easy ways to get a child into a productive mindset.

Key Points:

1. **Discuss returning to school with your children to get them ready.**
2. **Review expectations for the "new" year ahead of time.**
3. **Implement structure to help with success.**
4. **Make sure your children have an academic plan and can perform the required tasks.**
5. **If needed, get your child academic help early.**

6. **Mandate balance.**

7. **Help your children set up activities.**

8. **Take a family vacation.**

9. **Introduce mild academic material, i.e. "fun reading."**

10. **Give your child some freedom to relax and have fun.**

FAQ's

1. Should I mandate a structured routine for my child over the holidays?

Yes and no. You'll want to have structured activities whether it is camp or a planned vacation, but at the same time it is important to allow your children choice and participation in what those routines might be. For instance, if it is a camp, allow them to pick the kind of camp. You also want to allow kids to have time just to play, relax, and hang out with their friends, so their time "off" is balanced.

2. Is it okay to extend absence from school for family vacations?

It is never a good idea for children to miss too much school. On occasion, if your vacation runs over a day or two that is okay. However, remember that missing school constitutes being behind on assignments and other school events which might make your child feel anxious if they get back to school too late.

3. Should I let my children sleep in during vacation?

Despite feeling as though your children might be lazy and can sleep all day, it is important to also know that your children are growing and their bodies need sleep. Because of complicated and busy school schedules oftentimes they have to get up early and don't really have a day to sleep in, therefore doing so over vacation is okay to a degree. Sleeping all day is different than sleeping late. Again, assisting your child in balancing rest with activity is always a good idea.

4. ***My child works two jobs every summer with almost no free time. Should I insist they take some "vacation" time?***

Wow, what an industrious child you have! But again, balance is key. Remember that as parents we are trying to teach our children to balance fun with work. If there is too much of one over the other, something will suffer. Therefore, encourage your hard-working child, but remind them that summer vacation goes by pretty quickly. It might be nice to have a little time to relax and spend time with friends; maybe even a family vacation would be a nice break from working two jobs.

5. ***My child spends the entire summer at the beach. If she gets good grades during the school year, what expectations should I place on her over the summer?***

Just because it is summertime does not mean parents relinquish their job of both understanding a child's need for relaxation and having fun, and making sure their child doesn't get too far away from using their minds in more academic or creative means. It is always a good idea to balance their necessary beach time with some scheduled camps, lessons, or an activity that keeps their minds in shape for the next school year. Therefore, when the fall comes, they will not feel completely deficit. In addition, because school is not a daily factor, the summertime provides opportunities to learn new things which most children do not have time for during the school year, such as learning a musical instrument, taking an art class, or volunteering their time to help people. Not that this should be the predominance of the summer, but some mental stimulation and contribution is always a good idea during school breaks.

CHAPTER 23

GRANDMA'S HOUSE

LESS RULES AND MORE FUN: IF MOM SAYS "NO", GO ASK Grandma. These are some of the common adages associated with going over to Grandma's house. This is certainly the case for five year old Sophia. She visits with her grandmother every Saturday and is showered with candy, gifts, and activities. She can't wait to go and talks about it all week long. The visit is equally gratifying for her grandmother, who compares Sophia to likenesses of her daughter, Sophia's mother, at the same age. "It feels like the old days to me," states Grandma. But when the visit is over, Sophia's attitude changes and she becomes angry and impulsive once she gets back to her house with the daily routine and restraints. This "attitude" can last for hours to days, and is very stressful for Sophia's mother, Debbie. "Grandma's house is like Disneyland; she lets Sophia do whatever she wants, but the consequence is she is very angry once she gets home and back to a reality involving rules and expectations." Debbie has discussed her concerns with her mother about trying to be more consistent with her rules when Sophia comes to visit her, but Grandma does not want to be the disciplinarian.

Grandchildren are wonderful extensions of passing along family linkages. In many ways they are as pleasing as a second opportunity to raise children without the structure. Spending time with grandchildren brings back fond memories and experiences of parenting and reliving the old days of having young children around the house. It also keeps the grandparent feeling young and engaged. However, as a result of generational differences and personal experiences, differences often arise with regard to values and beliefs about how to best raise the children. For example, in some families, practices of discipline are consistent along generational lines; in other cases the parents of the child decide to change old patterns. Such distinctions can frequently cause conflicts between the parent and grandparent. Not only the conflict, but also the variety in styles of discipline can become confusing for the child if the practices are different in each household. Sophia's difficulty readjusting to her home is an example of just such confusion. In many cases, grandparents and parents disagree on ways to raise a child which results in verbal disputes and mixed messages that leave a child feeling caught in the middle. So, how can the grandparents and parents work together on behalf of raising the grandchild?

Key Points:

1. **Be mature and talk about beliefs regarding raising children without the child present.**

2. **Parents need to educate the grandparents on their parenting style, rules, and expectations.**

3. **Work as a team on behalf of the child to avoid making them feel confused.**

4. **When a concern about a parenting style arises, be sensitive when discussing it with the other party; reinforce that you are not trying to be critical, but helpful.**

FAQ's

1. *What if the grandparents refuse to adhere to my rules for my children?*

You will be in a lot of conflict. On the one hand you want your children to have a good relationship with your parents, but on the other hand you will not be happy when your parents aren't supporting your rules and ideas about what is in the best interest of your child. I always recommend talking to the grandparents privately about the importance of your rules and their helpfulness in supporting them. It will reduce conflict in the grandchild because they will not be hearing two different messages from the important people in their lives. However, if all attempts to align together fail, then you might have to be more present during those visits to make sure your rules aren't undermined.

2. *What if the grandparents give my child a gift of which I do not approve?*

The first step is to ask yourself why you do not approve of it. Make a determination if it is something you really don't like, or if you don't like the fact that it was given to your child by your parents. In some cases you might decide to allow your child to keep the gift because it was given from the grandparents, but you may have to place some restrictions if you feel it is inappropriate, such as a particular type of video game. If you feel the gift will be too conflicting to you as a parent, you will have to empathically explain that the gift was a nice gesture, but is not appropriate for the child's age, offering to return it and use the money to buy something they might like which is more age-appropriate.

3. *My spouse's parents speak ill of me out of my presence but do so directly in front of my children. What should I do?*

You should talk to your spouse about making it clear that these types of comments are not only inappropriate, but hurtful and harmful to your children. As adults, especially family members, we need to respect the love of a parent by a child, irrespective of your feelings about that parent. Otherwise you are creating discomfort for your child. In other words, keep your feelings to yourself about your in-law and vice versa.

CHAPTER 24

CHILDREN AND DIVORCE

ALTHOUGH THE DIVORCE RATE HAS DECREASED TO 41% over the past five years, divorcing parents are understandably worried about the effect this action will have on their children. During this difficult period, parents are plagued by their own problems, but continue to be and need to be the most important people in their children's lives.

While parents may be devastated or relieved by the divorce, children are invariably frightened and confused by this threat to their security. The age of the child when parents divorce is very significant. For example, the effects of divorce are less intrusive for young children. Children under the age of two usually do not understand the concept of divorce and adapt easier than older children who have bonded longer with their parents, and who are also able to better understand what might be in store for them as a result of their parents no longer being together. The children most affected by divorce are between the ages of 4 and 14. During these ages, both parents play an important developmental role in their child's life; consistent time with each parent is optimal. Parental fighting, custody issues, and the introduction of new adults into the child's life create conflicts and often intense anxiety. Loyalty conflicts commonly enter the picture where the child feels stuck in the middle, worrying how one parent will feel or act when the child spends time with the other. To further complicate matters, some parents feel so hurt or overwhelmed by the divorce that they may turn to the child for comfort or direction, placing the child in an unhealthy position.

Divorce can be misinterpreted by children unless parents tell them what is happening, how they are involved and not involved, and what will happen to them. For example, many children believe they have caused the fighting between their mother and father and assume the responsibility for bringing their parents back together, sometimes by sacrificing themselves. Vulnerability to both physical and mental illnesses can originate in the traumatic loss of one or both parents through divorce. With care and attention, however, a family's strengths can be mobilized during a divorce, and children can be helped to deal constructively with the resolution of parental conflict.

Parents should be alert to signs of distress in their children. Young children may react to divorce by becoming more aggressive, uncooperative, or withdrawing. Older children may feel deep sadness and loss. Their schoolwork may suffer and behavior problems are common. As teenagers and adults, children of divorce can have trouble with their own personal relationships and experience problems with self-esteem.

It is helpful to the children if they know their mother and father will still be their parents and remain involved with them even though the marriage is ending and the parents won't live together. Long custody disputes or pressure on a child to choose sides can be particularly harmful to a youngster and can add to the damage of the divorce. Research shows that children do best when parents can cooperate on behalf of the child.

The parent's mutual ongoing commitment to the child's well-being is vital. If a child shows signs of distress, the family doctor or pediatrician can refer the parents to a child and adolescent psychotherapist for evaluation and treatment. In addition, the psychotherapist can meet with the parents to help them learn how to make the strain of the divorce easier on the entire family. Psychotherapy for the children of a divorce, and the divorcing parents, can be helpful if deemed necessary. Talking to children about a divorce is difficult, but necessary. The following suggestions can help both the child and parents with the challenge and stress of these conversations.

Key Points:

1. **Do not keep the divorce a secret or wait until the last minute to tell the children.**
2. **Parents should tell the children together.**
3. **Keep things simple and straightforward.**
4. **Tell the children that the divorce is not their fault.**
5. **Admit it will be sad and upsetting for everyone.**
6. **Reassure your children that you both still love them and will always be their parents.**
7. **Do not discuss each other's faults or problems with the children.**

FAQ's

My colleague, family law attorney Garrison "Bud" Klueck, CFLS, has some additional thoughts about how children can have input into the divorce process. Following are his responses to pertinent questions on the subject.

1. *If what Dr. Kanner says is true, and divorce can totally affect and disrupt children's lives, how do children get their voices heard in the divorce process?*

To begin with, the reader needs to understand that when we talk about children and court, we are talking about them testifying in *Family Court.* The basic rule is that children *do not testify* in Family Court. They cannot even testify through written declarations or affidavits the way adults often deliver their input. This is different from children in Juvenile Court. Juvenile Court involves juvenile delinquency (minors committing crimes) or juvenile dependency (children possibly becoming wards of the state and being put into foster care). Children frequently testify in Juvenile Court.

2. *Well, if we know divorce has such a huge effect on children, but they don't testify at Family Court, how can the children get their points of view considered?*

There are basically three ways, two of which involve mediation at Family Court Services. All couples who have child custody disputes must participate in mediation at court through Family Court Services. Family Court Services is the state-authorized, state-financed mediation system. If the reader hears the terms "FCS," "child custody mediation," "court mediation," or "Family Court Services," all those terms mean the same thing.

Sometimes the FCS mediators talk to children. Ages 10 to 15 are the most likely to be interviewed by FCS. Children who are of "single digit" ages (9 or younger), generally are believed to be too young. Minors who are16 and 17 years old are mostly concerned with their peers and high school "stuff." If the children have been involved with mental health counseling, FCS mediators seem to love to talk to the counselors of children. This tendency is true for school counselors as well.

The third way for minors to have input is when the court appoints "Minor's Counsel." Minor's Counsel is an attorney who represents the child. Our office has been appointed many times by judges as minor's counsel. We have had minor clients as old as 17 years, 364 days (they no longer have minor's counsel once the minor becomes an adult), and as young as two hours old (the baby did not have a name yet but did have his own attorney).

3. *We know there are "non-court" ways of getting divorced. Do they have ways for children to have input?*

Yes. The three "non-court" methodologies are mediation, collaborative divorce, and cooperative divorce. All have mechanisms built into the process to hear from children. For example, collaborative divorce and cooperative divorce have actual positions of "child specialist" built into the system.

CHAPTER 25

THE IMPORTANCE OF FAMILY DINNERS

BUSY SCHEDULES, DUAL INCOMES, RESISTANCE OF ADOLESCENTS to talk to their parents about their lives, and many other factors have frequently led many families to abandon the tradition of family dinners. Some of the most valuable bonding time in a family occurs during dinnertime.

The truth is that in most families these days the only time a family can be together and actually visit with one another is during a meal. Depending upon the age of your children, especially if they are over the age of 6, they really do not want to talk much about their days and will "plead the 5th", basically remaining silent during the meal. Understandably, most parents feel frustrated and try to generate conversation out of interest and love for their children only to be rejected and hurt. This can lead to arguments, groundings, or even a decision to just forget about the family dinner idea altogether. If you have a child under the age of 5, they love to talk and could easily take over the entire dinner conversation all by themselves, which results in the older children rolling their eyes and asking to be excused.

So, what can families these days do to reinstate the family dinner tradition in an attempt to make it beneficial for all? I've had many parents share with me the idea of "taking turns" talking about their day, but if you have an adolescent in your home, the common response is "I'll pass." If you have a child between the ages of 7 and 11, the common language used to describe their day at school is "fine" without any details whatsoever.

The situation described is typical, normal, and frustrating for every loving and caring parent because they want to know how their children are doing and be involved in their lives. Even the best parent cannot read their child's mind; we need information from them to assess how they are doing. Report cards, progress reports, and other external means of information are helpful in knowing how a child is managing themselves, but they are not a substitute for personal interaction. Unless you have a very mature child, all parents have to be clever in how to get their child or adolescent to talk.

What you are doing with this mandate of engaging conversation during family dinnertime is: 1) reinforcing the notion of "family" despite developmental changes; and 2) communicating that you are interested in your child regardless of what they might be going through. Such a tradition will likely be passed down to their generation and hopefully the next. We need to get back to the basics by instilling family values in our children. Dinnertime may be the only time a family can all be in the same place at the same time without involving a movie or video game. Here are some of the basic ways to ease the tension around the dinner table.

Key Points:

1. **Institute family dinner time and mandate it at least three days a week.** During this time you at least have their attention and you as the parent are emphasizing the importance of "family time."
2. **Prepare meals the children enjoy.** This may be difficult if you have children at different ages, but it is worth the effort. If children enjoy what they eat, they will be in a better mood. Obviously, make it healthy, stay away from junk food items, and don't allow yourself to become a short order cook offering many different options during one meal.
3. **Be in a good mood yourself.** Begin by talking about your day and share some experiences with your significant other if you have to be the one to get the ball rolling. You could even consider making an agenda with your partner ahead of time covering topics which have to do with feelings (happy, sad, frustrating, etc.) to help model the importance of sharing and talking. Stay as positive as possible so it does not become a complaining hour and create negative feelings for the evening. Do not use this time to discuss misgivings about your children, for they will retreat immediately. Save those times for private moments.
4. **Do NOT interrogate children over 6 years old with questions such as "How was your day?"** Instead, bring up neutral topics, current events about their school, favorite sports team, etc.
5. **Consider inviting your children's friends to some of your dinners.** "Tween" and teen guests will often share all sorts of information with you that your own children will not because you are NOT their parent. You CAN ask these friends questions about school, friends, etc. They are more likely to answer because

they are not in the process of having to prove their independence to you.

FAQ's

1. *What happens if your children don't talk or refuse to talk at the dinner table?*

Don't interrogate them. They are not talking for some reason and it could be: 1) they are tired or in a bad mood; 2) they don't want to tell you too much about their life because they like their privacy; or 3) they may be afraid of what might be said if they do talk. So, what do you do? You make comments on their mood. For example, if they look sad, instead of asking them what's wrong you point out that they look sad. Oftentimes when children aren't questioned, but are recognized for their feelings, they will open up if nothing more than to tell you they are "just tired." The other successful way of getting children to talk and communicate at the dinner table is by focusing the conversations on neutral topics. That way everyone can equally contribute and all opinions are welcomed.

2. *How do I get my children to not interrupt each other at the dinner table?*

Take turns. Your family time is typically a battle for your attention. If you have more than one child then they are constantly competing to tell you about themself because they want you to notice and be proud of them. The savvy parent therefore understands this and given this knowledge of competition, will make sure to fairly allow each child time to speak whether it is by allotting time or taking turns. Equality at the table is important. If one of your children wants to pass their turn, that is fine, but make sure they know they can contribute anytime. They just need to ask.

3. How do I get my children to all participate in the same topic?

Introduce a subject everyone can relate to, one each person can independently have an opinion about. Then it becomes a question of sharing and coordinating the answers of all parties involved to have a constructive conversation. For example, introducing the concept of a family vacation, soliciting everyone's input on where they would like to go and what they would like to do, is the beginning step of designing a family vacation that has something for everyone. This approach allows for less anxiety and less stress, greater interest, and a greater likelihood that all family members will enjoy a vacation intended for the entire family's pleasure.

CHAPTER 26

PARENTAL INTRUSIVENESS

Fifteen year old Sarah thinks her mother is crazy. She tells her friends that no matter what she does her mother is always just around the corner watching and listening, squawking at anything she does that her mother deems inappropriate. Sarah feels trapped because on the one hand she understands her mother is trying to help and protect her, but on the other hand she truly believes her mother overreacts to everything considered normal for any other child her age. For example, Sarah is not allowed to check her Facebook account unless her mother is supervising her time on the computer. For Sarah this feels like a huge invasion of privacy, and given the fact that Sarah is a straight "A" student and a very responsible child, she feels humiliated her mother won't trust her to make good decisions while on Facebook and tweeting. It has gotten so bad Sarah refrains from using her own computer at her house and does all of her social media activities in school or at a friend's house to avoid feeling intruded upon by her mother. She has cried, yelled, and pleaded with her mother to give her more privacy and space, but her mother is relentless in worrying that something terrible will happen to Sarah if she doesn't continually keep her eye on her activities. Interestingly enough, Sarah has never had any problems socially or academically which would explain her mother's constant supervision. Sarah's mother's concerns seem unrelated to Sarah per se, having more to do with her mother's own generalized concerns about the influences of media and television on children, and her own bad experiences with internet dating. Her mother is not comfortable discussing her experiences with Sarah so instead she remains very protective of her.

Just how much should parents be involved, and at times, even violate the privacy of their children? If you ask healthy adolescents, most of them would either say "never" or "infrequently" while the "tweens" (11 to 12 year olds) might say "sometimes." The latency-aged children (ages 5 to 11) would be more open to ongoing parental participation and helpfulness. These results are based on differences in the developmental and maturational levels of children and adolescents. There is a natural need for children to desire independence and separateness from their parents in order to build a sense of autonomy and healthy self-esteem. Children and adolescents alike will express this need by making independent decisions, establishing a certain amount of privacy, spending an increased amount of time with peers rather than parents, and in addition, engage in activities different than those practiced by their parents. All this is an attempt to demonstrate they are growing up.

Engaging in activities different than those practiced by their parents often causes the most parental angst, i.e. a concern their children may participate in activities which could negatively influence their health and development. Experimentation with drugs and alcohol, poor study habits, poor choices of friends, sexual activity, and risks of internt usage t keep parents in a constant state of worry. To complicate matters further, as children move along developmentally, most no longer openly engage in dialogue with their parents, leaving the healthy parent worrying and wondering how well their child is managing their life. By late adolescence, the child reacquaints themselves with their parents, often in an even closer fashion than in the early years, but between late childhood and late adolescence, parents are often "the last to know" how well their child is managing his or her life.

Despite such realities, and although the developing child may seem covert, their behavior is quite observable to the attentive parent, especially if they are in some kind of trouble or in a difficult transition in their lives. Although there is a push towards independence and privacy, the child will have a difficult time containing all of their emotions and transitional states of mind. Symptoms, or signs of distress, manifest in every household when an internal conflict becomes too intense for the child or adolescent to manage on their own, providing a needed opportunity for parental assistance or intrusiveness. Such symptoms could include, but are not limited to, slipping grades, depressed mood, sleep disturbance, and obviously the use of drugs and alcohol, just to name a few. When such symptoms manifest themselves and the parent joins in to help their child through a difficult time, the result is generally positive. On the other hand, if the parents are either too far removed from an awareness of their child or become too involved, problems tend to intensify rather than rectify.

Taken together, the optimal role of the parent is to understand and promote healthy development by demonstrating good judgment and by implementing limits and helpfulness when needed (as determined by their assessment of the child's capacity to manage his or her life). Parents who balance basic limits to promote good choices and protect the welfare of their child while also allowing some choice and autonomy, tend to pave the road for a positive conclusion to the adolescent phase of development. They produce healthy and happy children. Regarding issues such as privacy, freedom, and independent choice, each parent needs to follow the research of what is "normal" developmentally in reference to the expression of feelings, thoughts, and actions, along with their own assessment of their particular child. Some children and adolescents are able to manage themselves better than others. The assessment is determined by external criteria such as their grades, work habits, and evidence of choice and judgment, combined with parental intuition. The child or adolescent who is more mature in these areas may be given more independent choice than the child struggling with self-management and appropriate judgment.

In optimal households, the childhood and adolescent years have normal peaks and valleys, highs and lows, all of which correspond to the developmental process. The parents who practice what I call "loving limits" seem to have the best outcome and their children, once they become adults themselves, seem to agree as well.

Key Points:

1. **Balance health, safety, and educational limits with some safe choices to promote autonomy and self-esteem.**

2. **Privacy is important as long as the child is not getting him or herself into trouble.**

3. **Parents need to be supportive of individual ideas and quests, guiding and leading toward future means of success.**

4. **If a problem arises, the parent needs to get involved and work with their child to repair the issue until it has vanished.**

FAQ's

1. *How do I know I can truly trust my child without spying on them?*

You don't know, but you base your consideration of trust on their behavior and achievement. For example, if your child is doing well in school, has good friends, takes care of himself and doesn't tend to make bad choices, you are probably going to feel more comfortable trusting him than if he is having problems with school, friendships, or other issues such as drugs. Parents need to be "on call" all of the time, not spying. On call means observing whether your child is managing themselves well enough without parental intervention. If you see your child slipping (which all parents do, even in the healthiest of times), your assistance in getting them back on track is essential.

2. *Do I need a reason to snoop on my child or is it good parenting to occasionally conduct random "quality control" checks?*

Parents need to be attentive and watchful, but that is different than snooping. In fact, if parents are aware and invested in their children's lives they will pick up on signs which indicate their child is having problems. For example, if a parent finds a beer can in their child's trash can, this would be an unconscious attempt of the child to alert the parent they are doing things that might not be in their best interest. It presents an opportunity for the parent to discuss the utilization of alcohol or other drugs and make it clear this is not condoned behavior. Such learning lessons are essential to keeping your child healthy.

CHAPTER 27

GETTING AND KEEPING CHILDREN IN SPORTS

MANY PARENTS ASPIRE FOR THEIR CHILDREN TO become invested in sports starting at an early age. Depending upon the particular background of the parent, this introduction can range from casual participation to one filled with expectation and pressure. Irrespective of the parental approach, the preferred outcome seems to be the same: the child develops a long-lasting investment in a sport which has both physical and psychological benefits. However, research demonstrates that if certain strategies are not followed from the beginning, the child can develop an aversion to sports and experience "burnout" at a relatively early age. This dilemma tends to happen under four conditions: 1) when the concepts of competition and winning are introduced too early in their development; 2) when skill acquisition is not emphasized, causing the child to develop "bad" habits; 3) when the sport activity is not initially and continually considered "fun"; and 4) when the choice of sport comes entirely from the parent and not the child.

Considering the first point, when children from ages 3 to 6 are encouraged to "compete" and "win" rather than play and have fun, conflicts over fears of losing and disappointing parents commonly arise. Stress and anxiety for the young child can cause them to participate in a sport for the sole purpose of impressing parents and avoiding feared rejection rather than because they want to learn something new and have fun. In many cases, when this occurs the child will eventually either reject sports altogether or play them for the wrong reasons.

With regard to skill acquisition, young children are still very much in the process of developing fine and gross motor skills. Usually, before the age of 6 or 7, they have trouble even successfully bouncing and catching a ball. Given these normal developmental limitations, when adults push too hard, the child is often faced with failure and subsequent negative feelings about themselves for not being able to perform to the level their parents believe they should be able to achieve. Furthermore, the child can also feel embarrassed that he or she is not performing well enough in front of others, once again making them feel badly about themselves. Although many pushy parents will make statements like "Just do the best you can", the young child is very much attuned to what they can and cannot do, and are unable to grasp such abstract concepts such as "Do your best."

Play should always be fun and enjoyable for young children who are invested in play as a way to learn and explore their world. When competitive or stressful conditions are introduced to children before they are developmentally ready to handle the challenge (which is usually between the ages of 8 and 10), the activity becomes stressful and more of an issue of "winning" or "performing" than developing an enjoyment and love for a sport. In addition, if time is not spent on teaching children proper ways of hitting or shooting a ball for example, poor habits develop which may limit the potential talent of the child for that sport. Young children are hungry to learn and when they are taught a sport in a fun and non-competitive manner, they tend to want to excel and continue to play the sport in the future.

Finally, it is very important young children are given a choice in the type of sport or sports they would like to learn. When the child is given some freedom, rather than a parent insisting they play a certain sport, the child feels it was their choice: this tends to increase the likelihood they will stick with that sport over time. Many parents who have backgrounds in a particular sport mandate their child play the same sport, and then become disappointed when he or she gives it up by adolescence. Without realizing that if their attitude was more relaxed, their child would probably naturally want to play the same sport as their parent as a subconscious means of relating to them.

In a nutshell, sports are a very important part of a child's development and help with both psychological and physical development. However, if caution is not taken from the beginning on how to introduce sports, many children will develop an overall aversion to sports in general and miss out on something which could be very rewarding for them.

Key Points:

1. **Avoid competition and winning for the first 8 years.**
2. **Work on good skill acquisition early to develop good habits.**
3. **Make it fun.**
4. **Give the child choices in the sport they want to play.**
5. **Help them feel good about their accomplishments.**

FAQ's

1. *My child hates sports; what should I do?*

Try to find out why he hates sports. Is it because he feels he is not good at sports, had a bad experience, or is afraid a sport is going to be too hard? Oftentimes when information is provided to a parent on why a child doesn't like something, steps can be taken and conversations can be held to assist the child in taking chances. However, if your child really doesn't want to participate, but you insist on him doing something active, it is best to allow your child to pick the sport. Oftentimes this compromise helps the child feel he has choices: he may better tolerate participating in his own choice of sport rather than hating all sports.

2. *How do I know when my child is ready to start organized sports?*

In order for children to begin organized sports they should have at least some basic physical maturational developmental skills such as some fine and gross motor coordination. In addition, the child needs to also understand the concept of rules and social interplay, namely that they are at a point in their development where they can play cooperatively with other children, rather than playing independently. If the child does not have these essential developmental milestones, then putting them into organized sports might not be a good choice and could even lead to a sense of inferiority in your child.

3. *How do I balance being my child's coach in a team sport?*

First, you must ask the permission of your child before agreeing to be a coach because you are putting your child in a position where he is seeing and experiencing you as someone different than his parent.

This can be very confusing for a child as he wants to feel special to you. The desire will intensify when he has to share you with a group of teammates. Such conflict for some children may be too much, but other children may manage it well. The most important aspect is to talk to your child before you agree to coach. Ask him questions such as, "How are you going to feel when I have to give my attention to other children? How will you feel if I can't make you first all of the time? How are you going to feel if I am not as good of a coach as others you may have had?" If your child seems to be okay with it, then signing up as a trial coach would be an important way of determining if this is something that will happen on a regular basis or not.

CONCLUSION

LOOK, LISTEN, RESPOND

PARENTING IS ONE OF THE MOST DIFFICULT, COMPLEX, and all-encompassing roles a person can ever have. It is important parents immerse themselves in trying to understand their child with empathy and guidance. Children need to be at the forefront of their parent's thoughts at all times. This is not to say mothers and fathers should not take care of themselves, but the primary role of a parent is to take care of the child which includes really working to help the child become a healthy functioning adult.

Engage in active parenting. You need to be an involved parent. Your position is to understand, encourage, protect, and guide. Always listen, always look, always respond when needed. When you listen to what your child is saying, ask yourself, "What are they trying to tell me?" Pay attention to them when you interact with them to get a gauge of how they are doing and how they are feeling. And always respond when they state something that might have an impact on their development or in their life. In other words, don't let them fail.

Keep in mind that children are not a complete package yet; they are still developing, so little mistakes along the way won't have a gross impact on them. However, anything such as not doing homework or being in a dangerous situation are risks parents should not take with their child's life. It needs to be explained to your child that the position of the parent is not to punish, but to help, to look out for and to protect. You are trying to help your child understand where their decisions are leading them. You don't just "trump" them — you talk to them.

I believe in setting "Picket Fence" limits: set a limit, set a fence around them, then let your child run. Picket Fence limits should be balanced between understanding the need for individual development (becoming autonomous), and protecting your child within established boundaries.

How much do you help a child? Only help a child as much as they need you to, both developmentally and functionally. You want to accentuate their capacity to do it; you don't need to do it for them. If they can't do it on their own then you help them as much as possible to take over the task.

As a practicing child adolescent and adult psychoanalyst I follow normal development as an underlying principle. Each phase of this development is based on specific tasks which need to be accomplished before a child, adolescent, or even an adult can move on to the next stage. Parents and parenting facilitate this process by helping guide children along the entire path. This is accomplished through a number of means; primarily through optimal parenting which models dynamic behavior, not just random acts. In other words, there are causes for everything adolescents and adults do which are based on their internal worlds as well as what happens to them on the outside. Changes are the result of insight and implementing appropriate ways of managing internal conflicts and outside dilemmas. It is my deepest desire to help parents to become great champions for their children. In doing so I know I will be helping their children become healthy, highly functioning adolescents and adults.

ABOUT DR. KANNER

Dr. Kanner is a Licensed and Board Certified Clinical Child, Adolescent, and Adult Psychologist and Psychoanalyst. Aside from a Full Time private practice in Rancho Santa Fe California, he is additionally an Assistant Clinical Professor of Psychiatry in the School of Medicine at the University of California San Diego where he teaches both human development and also trains medical students how to better understand and relate to their patients. He is also the Director of Clinical Counseling for La Jolla Country Day School in La Jolla California and is additionally a Clinical Professor at The San Diego Psychoanalytic Society and Institute.

Dr. Kanner has also been both an Expert Media Consultant for the past 10 years and 4 years ago launched his weekly television show, Your Family Matters, which he first hosted on Fox and is now on CW in San Diego. In 2008, his show won the IMedia Parenting Award for Television from Disney and his show continues to be one of the most popular ones in San Diego. Recently, Dr. Kanner was awarded Man of the year in Medicine and Healthcare by the ABA. Nationally, Dr. Kanner is one of the 15 LifeChangers for Extra TV in Hollywood where he gives advice to parents on raising children and adolescents and family life in general. In addition, has appeared on numerous television shows including: Dr. Phil; Fox and Friends; Geraldo; HLN; and Studio B to name a few. His weekly Blog that summerizes his weekly topic for television appears in newsprint in 5 different publications, including SDNN.

Dr. Kanner also sits on the National Board of Directors for Kids Korps USA which is the largest organization in the country which teaches children and adolescents the importance of volunteering to help the community at large. As a father of three children, he is also a dedicated baseball, football, and soccer coach.

CPSIA information can be obtained at www.ICGtesting.com
260770BV00005B/2/P

9 781934 509326